# CONSPIRACY

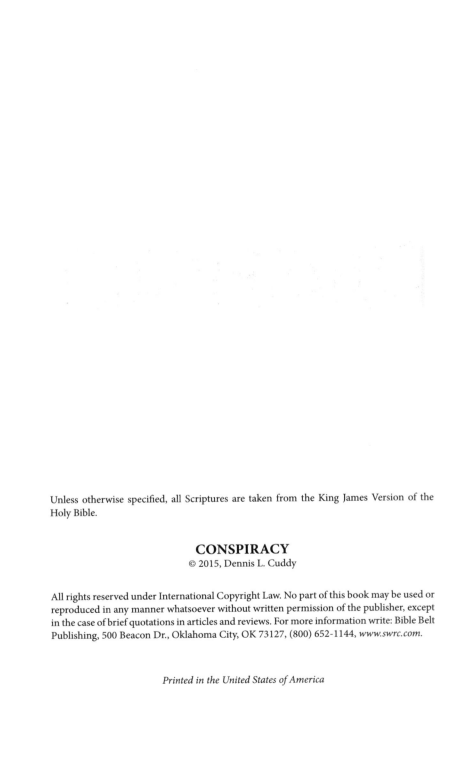

Unless otherwise specified, all Scriptures are taken from the King James Version of the Holy Bible.

# CONSPIRACY

© 2015, Dennis L. Cuddy

*Printed in the United States of America*

# CONSPIRACY

DENNIS L. CUDDY, Ph.D.

# Table of Contents

# Introduction

Have you ever wondered how people like H. G. Wells seemed to know what was going to happen? These people either had to be privy to the plans of the power elite (PE), or they were extraordinarily intelligent at figuring out what the secret cabal running the world had planned.

There is an ancient saying, "Ordo ab Chao" (Order Out of Chaos) that applies to the PE's machinations. And so as to make particular problems seen intractable, the PE selects global leaders who feign incompetence. This is one way in which the American public and others are manipulated. They are also manipulated and conditioned by things such as music and television.

The primary process used by the PE to accomplish its goals is the dialectic, using crises such as economic debt and wars, along with other coercive means. In the end, the public really doesn't have much of a choice when it comes to political candidates, and the PE controls both major political parties.

The latest major initiative to control the people is educational and called Common Core. I cover all of the above in *Conspiracy,* which is also the title of the next to last chapter herein, and takes the form of a conversation between a researcher and skeptic. Toward the end of this chapter, I even include specific examples of how I foretold of various terrorist activities. This is because someone once challenged me, saying that if my theory about a controlling PE were correct, there should be verifiable predictability.

Chapter 1

# How Did They Know?

In previous books and articles, I have mentioned that the power elite's (PE) global plan to bring about a world socialist government has been in operation for centuries. I have referred to Philip Freneau's article in 1792 explaining how they will gain control of the U.S., and will accuse anyone arguing against what they were doing as being against "the general welfare" (for which socialism purports to provide). And I have quoted from Alexis de Tocqueville's *Democracy In America* (1840) regarding how people will be "reduced to nothing better than a flock of timid and industrious animals." Shortly after this remark, in 1848, there occurred the first use of the term "new world order" when P. J. Bailey in the third edition of *Festus* wrote: "Ye are all nations. I am single soul. Yet shall this new world order outlast all."

Some time ago, I was talking with an Associated Press reporter about the PE's conspiracy to bring about a world government. He asked whether what happened over roughly the last century wasn't simply an organic evolution of events rather than a conspiracy. I replied that events didn't transpire organically if there was an organized plan and network carrying it out.

Just ask yourself how certain people knew things before they happened over the last hundred years. How could Stephen Wise write in his autobiography, *Challenging Years*, that in an address before the Trenton YMCA in 1910, he told them Woodrow Wilson would be elected New Jersey governor that year but not complete his first term before being elected president in 1912 and re-elected in 1916?

And relevant to World War I, how could the editor of *The Journal of American History* write that a leading political economist had recently said, "The most fearful war of the century is coming soon," in 1908? More specifically, how could Baha'i leader Abdul Baha be quoted in *The Montreal Gazette* on September 11, 1912, as stating that "the time is less than two years hence [when] a tiny spark will set ablaze the world," and World War I began the summer of 1914? And during the war, how could British King George at 11:30 a.m. on May 7, 1915, tell President Wilson's chief advisor, Col. Edward M. House, "Suppose Germany should sink the Lusitania with American passengers on board," and only two to three hours later Germany did exactly that?

Prior to World War II, how could H. G. Wells in *The Shape of Things To Come* in 1933 correctly predict that there would be a second world war beginning around 1939 and originating from a German-Polish dispute? And how could he also predict that the "modern world-state" (world government) would succeed on its third attempt (after the U.N. failed) about fifty years later, coming out of a conference in Basra, Iraq? More specifically, regarding World War II, how could Sir Julian Huxley, on December 5, 1941, state that he hoped that America and Japan would be at war "next week," and Japan attacked Pearl Harbor on Sunday, December 7, the first day of the next week?

But in perhaps the most telling prediction covering most of the twentieth century, how could Robert Hugh Benson in his 1907 *Lord of the World* say that "in 1917... Communism really began. ... [After 1989] the final scheme of Western Free Trade ... with the Release Act of 1998 ... there were ministers of euthanasia"?

Benson also referred to the "American socialism" and "free trade all over the world" to come.

How could all these people so accurately predict the future? Perhaps it was because the events they foretold were planned by the PE! For example, Benson's stepmother's brother, Henry Sidgwick, was a founder of the Society for Psychical Research (SPR) along with Cecil Rhodes' Circle of Initiates member British Prime Minister Arthur Balfour, and others. Additional influential SPR members have included Prime Minister William Gladstone, Lord Alfred Tennyson (who wrote about "the Federation of the World"), as well as the following Americans over the last century: William James, Mark Twain, John Dewey, Clarence Darrow, Margaret Mead, and New Ager Jean Houston.

With the world's future planned by the power elite, it is therefore no surprise that Arthur Calhoun in *A Social History of the American Family* in 1919 could describe the cradle-to-grave public education system to come in the American "socialist commonwealth." William Z. Foster would pick up on this in 1932 in *Toward Soviet America,* foretelling a National Department of Education with students taught "internationalism and the general ethics of the new socialist society. ... God will be banished from the schools." In the early 1960s, the U.S. Supreme Court banned Bible-reading and prayers in public schools. And in 1979, President Jimmy Carter established the national U.S. Department of Education.

At the time planned, in the 1980s, the Soviet Union suddenly stopped being referred to as "the Evil Empire" and was proclaimed our new friend, with the Soviet-American Exchange Agreement having Soviet educators come to the U.S. and help plan some of our schools' curricula. The dialectical materialism which William Z. Foster in 1932 said would be taught in our schools will be used to condition Americans to accept the dialectical synthesis of Western capitalism and Eastern communism into the world socialist government planned by the PE. As H. G. Wells wrote in *The New*

*World Order* (1939): "We are living in the end of the sovereign states. … In the great struggle to evoke a Westernized World socialism, contemporary governments may vanish. … Countless people … will hate the new world order … and will die protesting against it."

# Chapter 2

# Order Out of Chaos

(News with Views, March 27, 2006)

President George W. Bush often proclaimed how he brought "democracy" to Iraq. However, the "democracy" he brought there will result in sharia (Islamic) law being imposed. And in Afghanistan, where President Bush also brought "democracy," Associated Press reporter Daniel Cooney wrote "Afghan Man Faces Death for Christian Conversion," (*Washington Times,* March 20, 2006), which begins: "An Afghan man is being prosecuted [under sharia law] in a Kabul court and could be sentenced to death on a charge of converting from Islam to Christianity, a judge said yesterday."

From the beginning, Iraqi Shiites (who advocate sharia law) have cooperated with the American process of bringing "democracy" to that country because they believe that as the majority in Iraq, they will rule. But therein also lies the problem, because there is no incentive for them to compromise with Sunnis and others to form a unity government. If the U.S. threatens to withdraw its forces if the Shiites don't compromise, this might have little impact because the Shiites believe they would prevail in any possibly resulting civil war.

How did the U.S. get itself into such a dilemma? The Project for the New American Century (PNAC) under the leadership of

William Kristol long argued for Saddam's removal from power. And with members of PNAC holding key positions in the Bush administration, it was not difficult to get President Bush to invade Iraq. However, from the beginning, Kristol expressed his fear that the U.S. would try to win "on the cheap": with too few soldiers, resulting in the chaos which has existed since the invasion until today.

In an effort to understand why this happened, one should ask "Cui bono?" ("Who benefits?") from continued chaos in Iraq. The answer is the power elite. While President Bush was maneuvered into invading Iraq, the power elite's dialectical process persuaded the president (unrealistically) that he could achieve victory with only about 150,000 troops when his father deployed almost 600,000 against Saddam in 1991 just to remove Iraqi forces from Kuwait. There is no way 150,000 soldiers could occupy, secure, police, and nation-build a country the size of Iraq. Thus, continued chaos was assured.

Various explanations have been offered for the chaos. *New York Times* chief military correspondent Michael Gordon's new book, *Cobra II,* refers to the Bush administration's failure to anticipate the level of insurgency. However, in my book, *Cover-up* (published BEFORE the war began), I quoted exiled Iraqi Lt.-Gen. Tawfik al-Yassiri specifically referring to Saddam's planned guerrilla warfare. Moreover, in the new book *My Year in Iraq* by Coalition Provisional Authority administrator L. Paul Bremer III, he acknowledges learning of Saddam's strategy early in the occupation. Yet, President Bush still refused to increase troop levels. Not only did he not increase American troop levels, but he prevented the rapid training of Iraqi forces, which he claimed he wanted! Major-Gen. Paul Eaton was given the task of rebuilding the Iraqi army.

However, in Thom Shanker's article, "General Says Training of Iraqi Troops Suffered from Poor Planning and Staffing" (*New York Times,* February 11, 2006), one reads:

"We set out to man, train and equip an army for a country of 25 million—with six men," Gen. Eaton said. He worked into the autumn with "a revolving door of individual loaned talent that would spend between two weeks and two months," he said, and never received even half the 250 professional staff members he had been promised.

What the POE wants is continued relatively low-level chaos that wears people down and keeps oil prices high. In Greg Palast's March 20, 2006, article in *The Guardian* (London) about how "Bush didn't bungle Iraq," he refers to the State Department's secret 323-page plan for Iraq's oil in which was a "directive to Iraqis to maintain a state oil company that will 'enhance its relationship with OPEC.'" Palast went on to say that "every time the 'insurgents' blow up a pipeline in Basra, ... the price of oil leaps," and Big Oil loves it. In 2005, the top five oil companies made $113 billion in profit, compared to only $34 billion in 2002 before the Iraq war began.

The chaos in Iraq, the Middle East, and elsewhere, wears down Americans, Shiites, Sunnis, Israelis, Palestinian Arabs, etc., until all are willing to accept external control by global political, economic, etc., managers. These managers will bring a world government order out of chaos, which by that time all parties will accept because they will be too worn out to resist.

Therefore, President George W. Bush "stayed the course" of chaos, not because he was running things, but because he was "advised" that it would be "cowardly" not to continue his policy. President Bush was largely a product of the advice and information he was given and, just as important, NOT given. In other words, he was a useful pawn of the PE, just as was President Clinton. It's like Prof. Carroll Quigley said in *Tragedy and Hope* (1966):

The argument that the two parties should represent opposed ideals and policies, one, perhaps, of the Right and the other of the Left, is a foolish idea acceptable only to doctrinaire and academic thinkers. Instead, the two parties should be almost identical, so that the American people can "throw the rascals out" at any election without leading to any profound or extensive shifts in policy.

Remember that Prof. Quigley chose the word "Hope" in his book's title as referring to the power elite bringing to fruition Cecil Rhodes' plan "to take the government of the whole world."

At this point you may say nations of the world, such as the U.S., China, etc., would never submit to the PE. But what if there were another major terrorist attack? Or what if nations' computer systems "just happened" to fail? What if there were a flu pandemic and large segments of the population were forcibly quarantined? Or what if nations' crops "just happened" to fail because of weather modification? And what if nations "just happened" to have earthquakes? Remember Secretary of Defense William Cohen at an April 28, 1997, Conference on Terrorism said there are those who "are engaging in even an eco-type of terrorism whereby they can alter the climate, set off earthquakes [and] volcanoes remotely through the use of electromagnetic waves."

There is a psychology at work here. Do you remember in George Orwell's *1984* that Big Brother's agent, O'Brien, said that you will come to love Big Brother? It's like when the North Koreans tortured prisoners and then offered them some small kindness, the prisoners actually began to express their appreciation to the very people who had been responsible for causing their pain in the first place! They came to love Big Brother, and that's the PE's goal for each of us.

Alexis De Tocqueville in *Democracy In America* (1840) warned of what rule by the PE would mean:

Above this race of men stands an immense and tutelary power, which takes upon itself alone to secure their gratifications and to watch over their fate. That power is absolute, minute, regular, provident, and mild. It would be like the authority of a parent. ... It provides for their security, foresees and supplies their necessities, facilitates their pleasures, manages their principal concerns, directs their industry.... After having thus successively taken each member of the community in its powerful grasp and fashioned him at will, the supreme power then extends its arm over the whole community. It covers the surface of society with a network of small complicated rules, minute and uniform. ... The will of man is not shattered, but softened, bent, and guided. ... It does not tyrannize, but it compresses, enervates, extinguishes, and stupifies a people, till each nation is reduced to nothing better than a flock of timid and industrious animals, of which the government is the shepherd. ... It is vain to summon a people who have been rendered so dependent on the central power to choose from time to time the representatives of that power; this rare and brief exercise of their free choice ... will not prevent them from gradually losing the faculties of thinking, feeling, and acting for themselves, and thus gradually falling below the level of humanity.

Later, Prof. Quigley in *Tragedy and Hope* would say that the ordinary individual's "freedom and choice will be controlled within very narrow alternatives by the fact that he will be numbered from birth and followed, as a number, through his educational training, his required military and other public service, his tax contributions, his health and medical requirements, and his final retirement and death benefits."

Today, many Americans are just watching garbage on their TVs as our profits go overseas—Amoco's profits go to England, Purina's and Gerber's profits go to Switzerland, TransAmerica's profits go to The Netherlands, etc., as American companies are being sold to foreign enterprises. Sound recording industries are

97 percent foreign-owned; metal ore mining, 65 percent; motion picture and video industries, 64 percent; book publishers, 63 percent; plastic products, 51 percent; etc. About 80 percent of our port terminals are managed by foreign companies, and parts for our missiles are now made in China, with whom we may be at war someday. To most people, this would make no sense. But to the power elite, it makes perfect sense.

Remember that on March 10, 1962, Council on Foreign Relations member Lincoln Bloomfield presented Study Memorandum No.7, "A World Effectively Controlled by the United Nations" (under contract SCC 28270 with the State Department, headed by Rhodes scholar Dean Rusk), in which he wrote:

> A world effectively controlled by the United Nations is one in which "world government" would come about through the establishment of supranational institutions, characterized by mandatory universal membership and some ability to employ physical force. ... [But] if the communist dynamic was greatly abated, the West might lose whatever incentive it has for world government.

Of course, to get people to accept the world government the power elite has planned, patriotism must be diminished, and unsuccessful wars are very useful toward that end.

The PE's plan has existed for many, many years. In fact, note the reference to "military defeat" (unsuccessful war) in Philip Freneau's article, "Rules for Changing a Limited Republican Government into an Unlimited Hereditary One," in the July 1792 edition of *American Museum*. He warned that the power elite would emphasize the limitations of the American Republic's Constitution, with "precedents and phrases" (e.g., due process) "shuffled in." He next indicated that civil turbulence in the republic would be contrasted with the stability existing under the hereditary elite. The "grand nostrum" of Freneau's outline of the power elite's possible plan was the creation of debt "made as big as possible, as perpetual as possible, in as few hands as possible," and as complicated as possible. He then said, "A great debt will require great taxes. ... Money will be put under the direction of government, and government under the direction of money" (e.g., banking elite).

The next step would be to create "artificial divisions within society" (e.g., "divide and conquer" strategy) which would "smother the true and natural division between the few [elite] and the general mass of people, attached to their republican government and republican interests." Freneau then indicated that the elite would give a popular name, such as "the general welfare," to the usurped power so that those opposing the elite could be negatively labeled as "opposing the general welfare" of the people. He described how a military defeat (e.g., the Vietnam War) would be turned into political victory for the PE. And lastly, he noted that those warning about the elite's attempt to seize power would themselves be labeled as "enemies to the established government." Freneau declared that this charge would "be reiterated and reverberated till at last such confusion and uncertainty be produced that the people, being not able to find out where the truth lies, withdraw their attention from the contest." Doesn't this warning by Freneau sound like what the PE is doing today?

# Chapter 3

# Planned Incompetence?

In 1957, Egyptian president Gamal Abdel Nasser wrote: "The genius of you Americans is that you never make clear-cut stupid mistakes, only complicated stupid ones, which makes us wonder at the possibility that there may be something we are missing." What Nasser was close to asking was whether Americans (acting for the power elite) were operating with "planned incompetence," or PI. "Planned incompetence" is when a nation or individual seems to act in a mistaken way that indicates it doesn't know what it is doing, but it really does!

For example, Nasser came to power in 1952 as the U.S. was engaged in the no-win Korean War. You might ask why any nation would become involved in a war it didn't want to win. Although Gen. Douglas MacArthur was confident that we could win that war, he was blocked by President Harry Truman, who was a puppet of the power elite (PE), as are most world leaders The PE's goal is a world government, and on June 28, 1945, President Truman had said: "It will be just as easy for nations to get along in a republic of the world as it is for us to get along in the republic of the United States." And as Council on Foreign Relations (CFR) member Lincoln Bloomfield would later write, a "world government" would come about "through the establishment of supranational institutions, characterized by mandatory universal membership and some ability to employ physical force. ... [But] if the communist dynamic were greatly abated, the West would lose whatever incentive it has for world government." Therefore, since President Truman had helped bring the communists to power in China in 1949 (through Gen. George Marshall's denial of working weapons to the nationalist Chinese), he disallowed Gen. MacArthur's military action against the Chinese communists as the main supporters of communist North Korea.

In the same year (1952) that Nasser became head of Egypt, Herman Dinsmore became foreign editor of *The New York Times* until 1960, and wrote in *All The News That Fits* (1969) that "the weight of *The New York Times* has generally fallen on the communists since the end of World War II." This is perhaps one reason *The New York Times* didn't expose the fact that Cuba's Fidel Castro was really a communist. When Castro came to power in 1959, he was presented as only a freedom fighter. Several years later when he announced that he was a communist, it looked like the American government had simply been incompetent in not knowing he was a communist, when the fact was we knew he was a communist all along—another example of PI ?

In the mid-1960s, President Lyndon Johnson began to increase greatly our military presence in the Vietnam War, but it was once again conducted as a no-win war. Over 50,000 American soldiers were killed before the war was over, as we hadn't seemed to learn anything from the results of our no-win strategy in the Korean conflict. Actually, this apparent incompetence served the PE's purposes well. One of the lesser known founding fathers, Philip Freneau, in *American Museum* (July 1792) explained how losing wars would be part of the elite's strategy to regain control over the United States after our successful war for independence against the British.

Prior to the Vietnam War, patriotism was an important value among young Americans. However, pollster Daniel Yankelovich found that by 1973, only nineteen percent of college educated youth and only thirty-five percent of non-college educated youth between sixteen and twenty-five years of age thought patriotism is an important value. This great decline in the importance of patriotism was necessary for the PE to establish a world government under which national loyalties would be subsumed.

In 1979, the Shah of Iran was removed from power and replaced by the Ayatollah Khomeini, who would later have his supporters take over the American embassy in Tehran. President Jimmy Carter's failed attempt to rescue our embassy hostages looked like bumbling incompetence, but was it really? According to an April 30, 1980, "Foreign Report" by *The Economist Newspaper Limited,* what was actually occurring was a signal to the Soviets not to attempt to invade Iran! "Foreign Report" wrote that

> although to the rest of the world the American raid appeared to be a pitiful failure, the unreported circumstances of the raid demonstrated to Russia that the American armed forces are able to send a large force (very much larger than the tiny force that landed in Iran) into a remote area of potential conflict … with success. … The (American-Iranian) back up force already in place (before the raid) was extensive, numbering 2500-3000 men.

Was this also an example of PI?

During the 1980s, the new Soviet leader, Mikhail Gorbachev, promoted the concepts of *glasnost* and *perestroika,* exhibiting a spirit of openness and cooperation. The United States seemed naively to buy this new Soviet approach by entering into the Soviet-American Exchange Agreement in 1985, whereby Soviet educators would help to write some curricula for American schools, among other education initiatives. This appeared to be a mistake born of incompetence, because in 1931 Soviet theoretician Dimitri

Manuilsky, addressing the Comintern in Moscow, revealed: "One day we shall start to spread the most theatrical peace movement the world has ever seen. The capitalist countries, stupid and decadent ... will fall into the trap offered by the possibility of making new friends. ... Our day will come in thirty to forty years or so. ... The bourgeoisie must be lulled into a feeling of security."

However, this wasn't really incompetence, but rather part of the power elite's (PE's) plan for a synthesis of capitalism and communism into a world socialist government. Relevant to this, Ford Foundation president H. Rowan Gaither in 1952 told congressional Reece Committee research director Norman Dodd:

> Of course, you know that we at the executive level here were, at one time or another, active in either the OSS, the State Department, or the European Economic Administration. During those times, and without exception, we operated under directives issued by the White House. We are continuing to be guided by just such directives. ... The substance [of these directives] was to the effect that we should make every effort to so alter life in the United States as to make possible a comfortable merger with the Soviet Union.

In 1988, George H. W. Bush (Skull & Bones member) was elected president, and with his success in the 1991 Gulf War against Iraq's Saddam Hussein seemed headed for re-election in 1992. However, in what seemed to be an incompetent move, he went back on his "no new taxes" pledge and lost to Bill Clinton. Assuring Bush's loss, Ross Perot entered the presidential race, as Teddy Roosevelt did in 1912, and split the "conservative" vote—another example of planned incompetence? What happened was the PE needed the Democrat Clinton as president to persuade enough Democrats in Congress to pass NAFTA and GATT as part of the PE's ultimate plan for a global economy facilitating a world government.

In the April 1974 edition of *Foreign Affairs*, Rhodes scholar Richard Gardner had written that "an end run around national sovereignty, eroding it piece by piece, will accomplish much more than the old-fashioned frontal assault," and he then explained how GATT would help move nations toward "surrender of sovereignty" and "world government." President Clinton made Gardner an ambassador, and on June 22, 1993, wrote to the World Federalist Association (WFA), noting their past president Norman Cousins had "worked for world peace and world government," and he signed the letter, "Best wishes ... for future success." NAFTA and GATT passed under President Clinton even though a large majority of the American people opposed them, and the great majority of the decisions of the World Trade Organization (part of GATT) have gone against the U.S. More and more American jobs also started going overseas.

In 2001, George W. Bush (Skull & Bones member) succeeded Bill Clinton as president and, in an occurrence of seeming incompetence, failed to prevent the terrorist attack of September 11, 2001. The government was well aware of Project Bojinka (a plan to hijack airliners and crash them into the World Trade Center, etc.), and on August 6, 2001, President Bush received a memo saying Al Qaeda leader Osama bin Laden was determined to strike inside the U.S. Despite this warning, President Bush failed to have placed on standby alert at any of New York City's forts an Apache Longbow helicopter, which easily could have prevented the hijacked airliners from striking the World Trade Center. The result of this seeming "incompetence" was that the American people, according to the results of an ABC/*Washington Post* poll the afternoon of September 11, 2001, suddenly became willing to sacrifice some of their freedoms for security (as desired by the PE), thus accepting the Patriot Act and Homeland Security Act.

Two years later, President Bush in another move of apparent incompetence attacked Iraq in 2003 over the issue of weapons of mass destruction (WMD). Planning for providing security from crime, for electricity, etc., for civilian Iraqis was practically nonexistent. But was this another example of PI, as the attendant turmoil caused the Iraqis to request American military forces to remain there and to grant the United States the largest embassy in the region (which then became a high level surveillance post between Iran and its ally Syria)?

In 2008, the global financial crisis began as the Securities and Exchange Commission had waived the twelve-to-one leverage ratios for the five bigggest investment banks, which then leveraged forty-to-one, collapsing the world financial system. This paved the way for Barack Obama to become president in 2009 and move the U.S. more and more toward socialism, taking over General Motors, Fannie Mae and Freddie Mac, etc., along with the inevitable socialized medicine resulting from Obamacare. That the website for Obamacare enrollment didn't work is an example of "planned incompetence," and millions of Americans have already been informed that their current health insurance policies have been cancelled. However, they have been told they could receive subsidies for their new Obamacare health insurance policies. The result will be that whatever the federal government funds will be more and more government-controlled, in this case the American heathcare system and who lives and dies (death panels). During his first term as president, from 2009 to 2013, President Obama also engaged in other examples of PI, such as allowing the American ambassador to Libya and three others to be killed in an easily preventable terrorist attack, which is still under investigation. Could it be that the U.S. was involved in weapons flowing from Libya to rebels in Syria and Hamas in Gaza?

Then there is the Edward Snowden debacle beginning in May 2013, when a low-level NSA employee absconded with top secret information and then went to Hong Kong and afterward to Russia. That this was able to occur at all seems at first to be sheer incompetence, but was it really PI? There are several possibilities in this regard. First, the power elite doesn't want any one nation to be too independently strong, and therefore may have wanted to share American intelligence information with the Chinese and Soviets (remember H. Rowan Gaither's and Lincoln Bloomfield's remarks). Or, Snowden may be feeding the Chinese and Russians information we actually want them to have in order to give them a false sense of security. Or, Snowden's revelation that the NSA has been collecting private phone conversations of Americans may be the PE's means of conditioning the people (the frog in the increasingly hot water syndrome) to accept this invasion of privacy in the name of fighting terrorism, and later this private information can be used against these Americans.

Currently, the debt level supported by President Obama and Congress is unsustainable and within the next two years will lead to another finanacial crisis—another example of PI? This is desired by the PE to bring about the global devaluation of currencies, which will force the world's nations to accept a world currency in 2018. This is all part of the secret Nazi (meaning National socialism) plan, which is a subpart of the larger PE plan for a world socialist government, and PI has been an important component in facilitating its occurrence.

Finally, relevant to PI, there is what I call the "psychological probe." In this case, it is designed to see how well the PE has dumbed down the American people. If there were a way for terrorists to hurt severely the American people, the competent thing to do would be to develop a means of preventing it. Right? On the February 5, 2014, national evening television news, it was announced that security officials for the Winter Olympics were concerned that terrorists might try to use toothpaste tube bombs to bring down airplanes. The reaction to this of most Americans was a simple, "That's interesting," period!

These Americans have become so dumb, they didn't ask why

terrorists (who have already easily slipped into the U.S.) haven't already used such bombs in grocery stores, pharmacies, etc. here. Such attacks at random across the U.S., even though not killing many, would create a sense of panic and fear among all Americans going to such places.

Simply prescreening all toothpaste tubes wouldn't solve the problem, because such explosives could be placed in any tubes (e.g., heating rubs, cheese spreads, etc.) or jars (e.g., vasoline, cold cream, etc.). And if the American people have become this dumb, the PE wouldn't have to concern themselves about whether the people would ask if the incompetence of not developing a prevention strategy was planned or not!

# Chapter 4

# The Manipulation of Americans

Horatio Alger died in 1899. He was a writer of boys' stories about individuals of little means who worked hard and became successful in a land of opportunity. That, however, was before the United States became an increasingly closed and manipulated society.

As Horatio Alger was passing, Sigmund Freud's young nephew, Edward Bernays, was growing up and in 1928 became William Paley's chief advisor at CBS. In that same year, Bernays wrote *Propaganda,* in which he described how the public could be manipulated. The stock market crash came the next year, and in the October 26, 1935, edition of *National Message* (found at the New York City Public Library), one reads: "It was told to me by a heavyweight American financier before the crash came, that the crash was coming, that it would be permitted to run to the danger point, and that then, when the danger point was passed, it would be reversed by measures carefully prepared in advance to meet the situation."

The stock market crash broke the Republican Party, and Franklin Roosevelt was elected president in 1932. In 1940, he was challenged by Wendell Willkie, an internationalist who had been a registered Democrat until 1940, and whom polls showed was favored by only three percent of Republicans just seven weeks prior to the Republican Convention. On June 19, 1940, Congressman

Usher Burdick wrote in the *Congressional Record*: "There is nothing to the Willkie boom for President except the artificial public opinion being created by newspapers, magazines, and the radio. The reason back of all this is money. Money is being spent by someone, and lots of it." Thus, the power (monied) elite were the power behind both the Democratic and Republican candidates for the presidency, and the masses were being manipulated by something that would come to be called "groupthink."

The term "groupthink" would be used by William Whyte, Jr. in *Is Anybody Listening?* (1950), in which he described the "social engineering movement" as "a machine for the engineering of mediocrity. … It is profoundly authoritarian in its implications, for it subordinated the individual to the group." This confirmed what Sigmund Freud said in his *Group Psychology and the Analysis of the Ego* (1922), in which he quoted Gustave le Bon as stating: "As a part of the group, man regresses to a primitive mental state. His critical, intellectual ability and control yield to emotionalism, suggestibility, and inconsistency."

The year after Whyte's book was published, Bertrand Russell's *The Impact of Science on Society* was published and described how, through education, government "could control its subjects securely without the need of armies or policemen." The next year (1952), the National Training Laborotries (NTL) became part of the National Education Association (NEA), and in 1962, the NTL published *Issues In (Human Relations) Training,* in which the editors wrote that human relations or sensitivity training "fits into a context of institutional influence procedures which includes coercive persuasion in the form of thought reform or brainwashing." The book also includes information about "change agent skills" and "unfreezing, changing, and refreezing" attitudes. In 1964, Roderick Seidenberg's *Anatomy of the Future* describes how the masses of people could be controlled "by the ever increasing techniques and refined arts of mental coercion" to the level of mindless guinea pigs.

The effort, of course, was to program people to the point where behavior would be predictable. In *Democratic Dictatorship: The Emergent Constitution oif Control* (1981), Arthur S. Miller describes a "new feudal order" controlled by elitists, and he assesses that "dictatorship will come—is coming—but with the acquiesence of the people. ... The goal is 'predictable' man." Two years later, FDR's son, Elliott Roosevelt, wrote in *The Conservators* that "there are within our world perhaps only a dozen or so organizations which shape the courses of our various destinies as rigidly as our regularly constituted governments ... this unofficial council of the elite, the creme de la creme of global planners." Four years later, Arthur S. Miller wrote *The Secret Constitution and the Need for Constitutional Change* (1987), declaring that "a pervasive system of thought control exists in the States. ... The citizenry is indoctrinated by employment of the mass media and the system of public education, ... people are told what to think about. ... A new vision is required to plan and manage the future. ... Ours is the age of the planned society. ... No other way is possible."

In 1992, the public was told to think about "change." Democratic presidential candidate Bill Clinton said he wanted to be an "agent of change." Just as in 1940, the monied elite were the power behind both Clinton and President Bush, both of whom had been Council on Foreign Relations (CFR) members and Trilateralists. And even though statistics showed Clinton's state of Arkansas had done poorly in many areas, he won the presidency despite his many personal problems in the past and his opposition to the vast majority of Americans on important issues of the day such as a voluntary school prayer amendment and parental consent for minors' abortions. Even though Clinton's negative ratings in the polls were quite high, individuals responding to the polltakers often indicated that they felt it was time for a "change" (just as they had been programmed to say), though they seemed to have no consensus regarding exactly how "change" would make things better. More recently, Barack Obama campaigned for the presidency in 2008 with the themes of "hope" and "change."

Another word that has been drummed into people's minds over the past sixty years by the media and press is "McCarthyism." This term has been used to close off debate immediately whenever someone suggested that communists may have become a powerful force in this country. Even the Clinton campaign quickly used the word when someone suggested that he may have been monitored by the KGB when he went to Moscow at the height of the Vietnam War. But what the media and press did not tell the public was that the basis for Sen. McCarthy's assertions is now known to have been correct. Former *Washington Post* reporter Carl Bernstein (of Woodward and Bernstein "Watergate" fame) in 1989 wrote *Loyalties: A Son's Memoirs,* in which he quoted his father (who along with Carl's mother were members of the Communist Party in America):

> You're going to prove McCarthy right, because all he was saying was that the system was loaded with Communists. And he was right.
>
> You've got to take a big hard look at what you are doing because the whole fight against his was that people weren't Communists. I'm worried about the kind of book you're going to write and about cleaning up McCarthy. The problem is that everybody said he was a liar; you're saying he was right. ... I agree that the Party was a force in the country.

According to communist theoretician Antonio Gramsci, one of the best ways to undermine a country like the United States was to attack the culture. Today, one can observe our culture being attacked via the media. On a recent episode of the popular television network program "Castle," the character Richard Castle (a writer) is talking with his 19-year-old daughter, who has decided to move in with her boyfriend. Richard protests, but his daughter reminds him that at nineteen, he moved in with his girlfriend. He pathetically replied, "That's different," and the daughter typically responds, "How?" Richard's partner in crimefighting, a police woman, tells Richard that her father objected when she first moved in with a boyfriend (clearly indicating she did it more than once). She then said the only thing her father's objection caused her to do was to be all the more determined to do it! Note that nowhere in that conversation was the fact mentioned that *The Holy Bible* in Galatians 5:19–21 says fornicators go to Hell forever. This is but one of many examples of how Americans today are being manipulated away from a biblical morality and into accepting a secular humanist morality.

Chapter 5

# Conditioning by Music

We know that music can have a profound effect on people. Certain types of music can have a calming or soothing effect. However, according to Oliver Sacks (Professor of Neurology and Psychiatry at Columbia University Medical Center), "music of a particular sort can actually trigger seizures." [http://www.pbs.org/wgbh/nova/body/sacks-musical-minds.html]

In Plato's *Republic,* he stated that "the introduction of a new kind of music can alter the character of a nation." The modern assault upon traditional American moral values began with the permissiveness of the Roaring '20s (e.g., look at the lyrics of the popular 1921 song "Sheik of Araby"). I have previously quoted from Antonio Gramsci, John Dewey, and Edward Bernays concerning their roles in altering societies and values, and here I'll focus on the role of music in this regard.

After the Roaring '20s, in 1934, the bisexual Cole Porter introduced a popular musical and song by the title "Anything Goes," which was about a shift away from restrictive codes of conduct. And in 1936, Irving Berlin composed the music and lyrics for the motion picture *Follow the Fleet,* starring Fred Astaire and Ginger Rogers, in which she sang "Let Yourself Go." In that same movie, Harriet Hilliard (later to be Harriet Nelson of "Ozzie and Harriet" TV fame) sang a song with the following lyrics:

Get thee behind me, Satan… but the moon is low and I can't say "no." … Get thee behind me, Satan, but the moon is low and I may let go. Get thee behind me. Someone I'm mad about is waiting in the night for me, someone that I mustn't see. Satan, get thee behind me. He promised to wait, but I won't appear, and he may come here. Satan, he's at my gate. Get thee behind me. Stay where you are. It's too late.

The message is clear—resistance to temptation is futile (also look at the lyrics of the popular 1942 song "That Old Black Magic").

Two years after *Follow the Fleet,* in February 1938, Theodor Adorno (formerly of the Frankfurt School in Germany) was made chief of the music division of Princeton University's Radio Project, which was funded by the Rockefeller Foundation. Adorno believed that repetition in music and other areas could create popularity, and that one could change the culture away from "the authoritarian personality" (belief in traditional authority) toward the "revolutionary," liberating individuals from traditional values. He also believed that the mass media could be used for "opinion management."

In 1941, Adorno left the Radio Project and moved to the University of California in Los Angeles where he taught for seven years, teaming with Max Horkheimer in 1947 to author *Dialectic of Enlightenment.* Horkheimer was director of the Frankfurt School during the 1930s and believed that authority within the family structure was a serious problem to be eliminated. In 1947, he also authored *Eclipse of Reason,* and in 1950 Adorno authored *The Authoritarian Personality,* indicating that those who emphasized their family, nation, or race actually had a psychiatric disorder. Adorno also theorized that an emphasis on fractious music could help destabilize society.

In 1951, Ohio disc jockey Alan Freed invented the phrase "rock & roll," which had sexual connotations. "Rock & roll" placed a heavy emphasis upon the beat and rhythm, and famous composer and conductor Dimitri Tiomkin would later judge that "the big beat is deliberately aimed at exciting the listener. There is actually very little melody, only rhythm. ... We seem to be reverting to savagery. ... Youngsters who listen constantly to this sort of sound are thrust into turmoil. They are no longer relaxed, normal kids." Tiomkin's analysis was supported by Aldous Huxley's statement in his *The Devils of Loudun* (1952):

> If exposed long enough to the tomtoms and the singing, every one of our philosophers would end by capering and howling with the savages. ... Assemble a mob of men and women previously conditioned by a daily reading of newspapers; treat them to amplified band music, bright lights ... and in next to no time you can reduce them to a state of almost mindless subhumanity. Never before have so few been in a position to make fools, maniacs, or criminals of so many.

In 1933 in *The Shape of Things to Come*, H. G. Wells had foretold of growing criminally infected areas after WWII (he said the war would begin in about seven years).

Scientifically supporting what Tiomkin and Huxley said, in 1957 Dr. William Sargent, former president of the Section of Psychiatry in the Royal Society of Medicine (London) authored *Battle for the Mind: The Mechanics of Indoctrination, Brainwashing, and Thought Control,* revealing

> that electrical recordings of the human brain show that it is particularly sensitive to rhythmic stimulation by percussion and bright lights. ... Certain rates of rhythm can build up reportable abnormalities of brain function and explosive states. Furthermore, it is easier to disorganize the normal function of the brain by attacking it simultaneously with several strong rhythms played in different tempos.

Sargent then stated: "Belief can be implanted in people after brain function has been sufficiently disturbed by accidentally or deliberately induced fear, anger, or excitement. Of the results caused by such disturbances, the most common one is temporarily impaired judgment and heightened suggestability."

Three years later, The Beatles formed in 1960 in a transition from "rock & roll" to "rock" music, and by 1967 their "Sgt. Pepper's Lonely Hearts Club Band" album had definite drug implications (even the U.N. Bulletin on Narcotics warned about it). In 1962, the Rolling Stones formed and are even popular today, despite producing such songs as "Sympathy for the Devil" and albums such as "Their Satanic Majesties Request."

The mid-1960s became a period of increasing revolution against traditional values. In 1964, The Who formed, and one of its members has proclaimed: "What we dish out is the musical equivalent of war—war upon quiet, war upon dullness, war upon certainty and stability." That same year, Mothers of Invention formed, and Frank Zappa, its leader, said, "The loud sounds and bright lights of today are tremendous indoctrination tools." The next year (1965), Jefferson Airplane formed, and member Paul Cantor revealed: "The new rock music is intended to broaden the generation gap, alienate parents from their children, and prepare young people for revolution." The next year (1966), Crosby, Stills and Nash met (formally forming in 1968), and David Crosby in *Rolling Stone* (Vol. 1) remarked: "I figured the only thing to do was to steal their kids. I still think it's the only thing to do. By saying that, I'm not talking about kidnapping. I'm just talking about changing young people's value systems which removes them from their parents' world effectively."

One important area of American values under attack in the 1960s was religion. Traditional biblical values were undermined and replaced by those of the religions of secular humanism and the New Age. Songs expressing the situation ethics attitudes of "do your own thing" and "if it feels good, do it" promoted the religion of secular humanism. And in 1967, the musical *Hair* opened and included the popular song, "Aquarius," which promoted the New Age religion. It contained the following lyrics:

> When the moon is in the seventh house,
> And Jupiter aligns with Mars,
> Then peace will guide the planets,
> And love will steer the stars.
> This is the dawning of the Age of Aquarius!
> Harmony and understanding,
> Sympathy and trust abounding,
> No more falsehoods or derision,
> Golden living dreams of visions,
> Mystic crystal revelation,
> And the mind's true liberation.

In 1969, the singing group The Fifth Dimension released this song as a single. And in the 1996 theosophical/New Age book *The Light Shall Set You Free* (theosphists believe Lucifer, "The Light-Bearer," sets one free as opposed to the biblical statement "the Truth [Jesus] will make you free") by Norma Milanovich and Shirley McCune, one reads: "The date for entry into the Fifth Dimension [when the Piscean or Christian Age will end and the Age of Aquarius will begin] is scheduled for the year 2012."

With the undermining of biblical values through music, it was therefore not surprising that the year after "Age of Aquarius" was released as a single in 1969, Perry Como in 1970 recorded "It's Impossible" which became very popular despite its lyrics, "I would sell my very soul and not regret it." Similarly, in 1977 Debbie Boone recorded the popular "You Light Up My Life," with the lyrics, "It can't be wrong when it feels so right," intimating that how one feels about a female-male relationship is more important than whether it might otherwise (e.g., morally) be wrong.

In the late 1960s and through the 1970s, rock music was followed by "hard rock." Writing about this in *Crisis in Christian Music* (2000), Dr. Jack Wheaton explained that "the repetitive, constant loud backbeat" of the drummer, "the pulsating (at an ear-splitting level), low-frequency vibrations, and the soaring, wailing, crying sounds of the amplified guitar trigger major subconscious emotional responses in the body, primarily stimulating aggressiveness, as well as providing increasing, but difficult to control, energy." He further related that when this music triggers the listener's fight-or-flight response, "the body is actually getting 'high' on its own internally-produced drug (adrenaline), resulting in… an increased tendency to aggressive and anti-social behavior."

According to Dr. David Noebel, this type of music has harmonic dissonance and melodic discord, which violate man's natural body rhythms. And Dr. John Diamond, a New York City psychiatrist, some years ago studied beats of over twenty thousand recordings and concluded "that a specific beat ('stopped anapestic rhythm,' which is contrary to our natural body beats and rhythms) found in over half of the top hits of any given week can actually weaken you. … It interferes with brain wave patterns causing mental stress."

With the introduction of "hard rock" in the late 1960s, there was a change in American values. Popular songs like the Rolling Stones' "Under My Thumb" and their later album cover for "Black and Blue" demeaned women. There was a corresponding dramatic rise in homicides and suicides from the late 1960s and through the 1970s in the U.S. In 1970, the popular movie *M\*A\*S\*H* was released with the even more popular TV series beginning in 1972. The theme song for the movie and series is actually titled "Suicide Is Painless," and elementary school children in the U.S. were taught both the music and lyrics, which inform students that "cheating is the only way to win, the game of life is lost anyway, and suicide is painless."

Musical promotion of violence continued into the 1980s with groups like Guns N' Roses formed in 1985. Its 1988 album "GN'R Lies" includes the lyrics "I used to love her but I had to kill her." GN'R (known for its cursing) also has an album with a rape scene on it! The year after "GN'R Lies" was released, the *Journal of the American Medical Association* (September 22, 1989) contained a report titled "Adolescents and their Music" warning that teenagers' fascination with heavy metal music may be associated with premarital sex, drug use, and satanic activities.

Given all of the above, it was not surprising that Tipper Gore in the January 8, 1990, edition of *Washington Post* wrote: "A majority of children surveyed by a Rhode Island Rape Crisis Center thought rape was acceptable. In New York City, rape arrests of 13-year-old boys have increased 200 percent in the past two years." A few months later in mid-July 1990, a landmark trial began in Reno, Nevada, regarding the British heavy metal rock group Judas Priest (formed in 1969) allegedly having a subliminal message, "do it, do it," on their album "Stained Glass," which supposedly led to the suicides of two teens who chanted "do it, do it, do it," before they shot themselves after hearing the album. One of the teens survived long enough to say it was as though the music controlled his actions, leaving him without a free will. He also remarked, "It was like a self-destruct that went off. We had been programmed." Wilson Key, a Reno experimental psychologist and author of four volumes on subliminal messages, testified that the misspelled word "sucide" is hidden on the cover of the Judas Priest album. The ability to control someone's "will" sounds like science fiction, but Dr. Robert Assagioli (who was a disciple of Luciferian occultist Alice Bailey), the founder of pyschosynthesis, believed it is actually possible to train the "will."

Through the 1990s as heavy metal rock music was affecting our youth, evidence mounted regarding its deleterious effects. Earlier research at Temple Bell College in Denver had already indicated rock music could even kill plants within a month. Then, in the August 10, 1997, *Washington Times* article "Heavy Metal Makes Killer Mice," one reads about research by David Merrel. According to the article, Merrel reported that "it was like the music dulled their senses. It shows point blank that hard rock music has a negative effect all around. I had to cut my project short because the hard-rock mice killed each other. None of the classical mice did that at all!"

Through the 1990s and into the twenty-first century, violence in music continued. The headline in the May 18, 2009, *Detroit News* read: "Eminem is the hottest ticket in town," even though the rap artist Eminem has sung about violence (e.g., murder, rape, etc.) against women.

Kimberly Smith in *Music and Morals* (2005) has explained that what is going on in music today is about "control." Traditional music, including traditional Christian music, is characterized by self-control, but rock music, including "Christian rock," causes a loss of self-control.

Music has been used to destroy our traditional biblical values, conditioning us to abandon self-control over our emotional impulses. And often the conditioning mechanism isn't obvious. The ABC News report, "Drug Drenched Lyrics No Music to Parents' Ears" by Carla Williams (ABC News Medical Unit) [http://abcnews.go.com/Health/Drugs/story?id=3834236] quotes, "Coke and rum; got weed on the ton," and says "So chime the lyrics of one of rapper 50 cents top singles in 2005. And such provocative messages, including those about alcohol and drugs, may well constitute a dominant theme in popular music." The report then indicated that Brian Primach at the University of Pittsburgh School of Medicine and Prof. Lisa Merlo in the Division of Addiction Medicine at the University of Florida "agreed that these messages have potential to sway behaviors in younger listeners." The report revealed that seventy-seven percent of rap music songs mentioned the use of illicit substances and thirty-seven percent of country music songs studied made such references.

These types of popular songs help destroy the moral values of our nation. And once our moral values are destroyed, we will then descend into chaos and ruin just like all past civilizations that lost their moral bearings.

# Chapter 6

# Secularism and Television

In 1928, William Paley was beginning CBS and hired Sigmund Freud's nephew, Edward Bernays, to be his chief advisor. In that same year, Bernays' book, *Propaganda*, was published showing how the American public could be manipulated. This "Father of Public Opinion," as Bernays was known, wrote: "Those who manipulate the organized habits and opinions of the masses constitute an invisible government which is the true ruling power of our country." He went on to explain that a politician could use a businessman's skills, taking "a survey of public desires and demands" and say, "I must lead the people. Am I not their servant?" This sounds a lot like Ross Perot in the 1992 presidential campaign.

And how is television used to manipulate the public? Dr. Robert Assagioli, founder of psychosynthesis and lifelong friend of occultist Alice Bailey (he was one of the "disciples" referred to in her *Discipleship In the New Age*), believed it is actually possible to train the "will." In that regard, Prof. Willis Harman of Stanford University indicated that a person's behavior is governed far more extensively than we realize by the unconscious or subconscious mind.

And Benjamin Libet, a professor of neurophysiology at the University of California, San Francisco, some years ago in the scientific journal *The Brain and Behavioral Sciences* said, "The conscious mind doesn't initiate voluntary actions." Monitors revealed that about a half-second before a muscle flexes, for example, an unconscious part of the brain sends signals seemingly to prepare the conscious part of the brain for action. Libet said that the conscious part of the brain can veto the unconscious signal, but the question is, "What if the person's 'will' has been conditioned not to veto the signal?" What if the person has seen the Nike slogan "Just do it" so many times that he or she "just does it"—whatever "it" is?!

In the last few decades, there has been an increase in the number of TV ads that show flashing lights and quickly changing images. In Aldous Huxley's *The Devils of Loudun* (1952), he explained that techniques like these could be used to manipulate the masses. The process, according to Bill Strittmatter, works something like this. Though most of life's events are normal, our survival instinct causes us involuntarily to focus upon "highlighted moments" (e.g., a gun firing, a car screeching, a phone ringing). In the new TV ads over the last several decades, there are a number of "highlighted moments" per minute.

These may be zoom-in close-up shots of faces, flashing images of the product to be sold, etc. Your mind is involuntarily immersed in these quick changes, simply digesting the image. And because of this mental process, you cannot simultaneously engage in conscious objective thought and analysis about what you are seeing. You simply absorb the information in a manner similar to someone being hypnotized. And instead of the brain registering the sight (or mention) of a product only a few times as during a traditional thirty-second or sixty-second commercial, the flashing newer TV ads with quickly changing images may cause the brain to register the name of the product many times during the same thirty-second or sixty-second time period. Side effects from these types of ads are not only stress in viewers, but also a decline in attention span, and hyperactivity in children (many children begin to complain of being "bored" when not watching TV).

Many middle-aged people and most of those older might be "turned off" by flashing lights and quickly changing images, but the younger generation accustomed to MTV music videos find it attractive. About the mid-1980s, many individuals in MTV began to move into commercial advertising. So what we are now witnessing is a concept which was developed that no longer appeals to reasons viewers should buy a particular product, but rather through quickly changing images shows a lifestyle with which a target audience associates. For example, a "cool" rapper might affect a target audience by pounding them with "Just do it" over and over again while numerous flashing images of Nike shoewear are registered in their brains. It is a powerful psychological technique.

Television can also manipulate people not only by what it shows them, but also by what it keeps from them. For example, before Russian leader Vladimir Putin guaranteed Syrian leader Assad's chemical weapons would be turned over, hardly a day would pass that the media would be showing the signs of atrocities committed by Assad's forces. However, now there is hardly a mention of the fighting taking place in Syria. The fighting hasn't stopped. It is just that the media now chooses not to cover it.

The only things the social planners and social engineers of the coming Brave New World Order fear are the negative exposures of their activities and plans, as well as organized opposition to their power and position of authority. As Edmund Burke said in his essay, *Thoughts on the Cause of the Present Discontents* (April 23, 1770): "When bad men combine, the good must associate, else they will fall one by one, an unpitied sacrifice in a contemptible struggle." And by "organize," I not only mean at the local level, but also at the national level. This is because a question has arisen as to the following. When the issue of "family values" was raised before the 1992 elections, there was plenty of time for the leading national conservative organizations to join forces and have the largest pre-election "Rally for Family Values" in Washington, DC that this nation has ever seen.

But they failed to do that, and they even failed to join forces to have rallies in state capitols. Because of the lack of initiative by national conservative leaders, the social issues (e.g., support for voluntary school prayer, and opposition to abortion, pornography funding, forced busing, etc.) were put on the back burner during the campaign and presidential debates. The same could be said for every election since then, but it has been these social issues that have provided the margin of victory for conservative politicians in our recent past. It is therefore absolutely essential that we organize and prayerfully as well as peacefully do that which is necessary to resist the principalities and powers driving our nation and others toward the New World Order and eventually the Antichrist.

A perfect opportunity to do this now presents itself regarding television with the scheduled Fox series "Lucifer" to begin in 2016. The series was picked up on May 9, 2015, and will focus on Lucifer, "who is bored and unhappy as the Lord of Hell and resigns his throne … to help the LAPD [Los Angeles Police Department] punish criminals." In the series, Lucifer runs a nightclub named Lux, has a lover named Maze, and a therapist named Linda, etc. Let's see if national religious and political leaders organize against this positive portrayal of Lucifer (Satan).

Chapter 7

# The Power Elite
# and Dialectical Process

## Caution: The Dialectical Process at Work

Richard Cummings in *The Pied Piper* described the activities of Allard Lowenstein (who worked with the CIA) in Africa, Spain, and Portugal. One of the important points he made was that while outwardly the U.S. government was opposing Marxists in Africa, behind the scenes the CIA actually was befriending (funding) them in order "gradually" to control them or at least cause them not to be so radical. What this actually revealed was the dialectic at work, and South Africa has played an important part in this.

In 1891, gold and diamond magnate Cecil Rhodes in South Africa formed his secret Society of the Elect "to take the government of the whole world." Part of Rhodes' plan involved selecting Rhodes scholars (e.g., Bill Clinton), and among the members of the Rhodes Trust was the famous author Rudyard Kipling who had swastikas on his early books. On the next page is reproduced a 1902 letter (note the suggestive words) from Kipling in Capetown, South Africa, to noted author H. G. Wells, who was one of the early Fabian socialists, with whom Rhodes' people networked. The Fabians wanted "gradually" to move Britain toward socialism.

At the same time Rhodes was developing his plan, William Whitney of the secret society Skull & Bones developed a plan financially to contribute to both major political parties, Democrat and Republican, and then have them alternate power so the public thought it had a choice when it really didn't. This would be in line with the "hope" of Bill Clinton's mentor at Georgetown University, Prof. Carroll Quigley, who authored *Tragedy and Hope* (1966) using "secret records" regarding Rhodes' plan.

Rhodes' people and members of Skull & Bones, all originally

well-off financially, have networked with Marxists/socialists "gradually" moving the world toward socialism dialectically, playing political liberals against political conservatives who alternate power. This is why there is a 1911 political cartoon by Robert Minor in the *St. Louis Post-Dispatch* showing men of wealth (e.g., John D. Rockefeller, J. P. Morgan, etc.) welcoming Karl Marx (with a book titled *Socialism* under his arm) to Wall Street.

Not long after this cartoon appeared, Marxist theoretician Antonio Gramsci began promoting his plan "gradually" to capture the cultures of countries rather than taking them over by violent revolutions. This idea of transforming whole cultures fit with Jan Christiaan Smuts' concept of holism. Smuts (along with Sir Abe Bailey, Sir Patrick Duncan, Basil K. Long, Richard Feetham and Sir James Rose-Innes) belonged to Rhodes' Association of Helpers in South Africa. Note the reproduced December 29, 1918 (next page), letter from Smuts to H. G. Wells stating "The next step is to move the political big wigs forward." In his book, *Holism and Evolution* (1926), Smuts described "the foundations of a new order of the universe." He drafted many clauses of the League of Nations, and was one of the drafters of the preamble for the United Nations Charter.

Shortly after Smuts' book was published, H. G. Wells in 1928 wrote *The Open Conspiracy: Blue Prints for a World Revolution.* In Wells' *Experiment in Autobiography* (1934), he described the goal of the "Open Conspiracy" as

an adequately implemented Liberal socialism, which will ultimately supply teaching, coercive and directive public services to the whole world, is the immediate task before all rational people. ... Plans for political synthesis seem to grow bolder and more extensive. ... The New Plan in America to the New Plan in Russia and how are both related to the ultimate World-State? There must be a common faith and law for mankind. ... Only

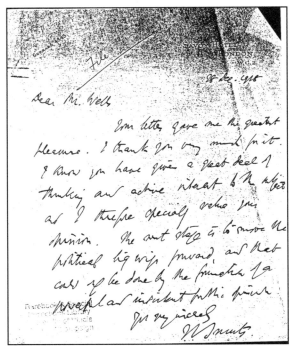

after a huge cultural struggle can we hope to see the world-state coming into being.

The ultimate goal of the PE is a synthesis of Western capitalism and Eastern communism into a world socialist government. Powerful financiers had funded the Soviets and in the 1930s funded Hitler's Germany. In 1936, PE representative John J. McCloy (Council on Foreign Relations chairman 1953–1970) would sit in Hitler's box at the Olympics and in late July 1961 take a friendly swim with communist leader Nikita Khrushchev in the Black Sea.

Just as the Soviets had been funded by the PE, the communist Chinese were brought to power by them as well. Actions taken by U.S. Gen. George Marshall after the Second World War helped the communist Chinese defeat the nationalist Chinese forces of Chiang Kai-shek, whom the U.S. was supposed to be supporting.

The communist victories in the Soviet Union and China were important to the PE. According to a 1952 map by the World Association of Parliamentarians for World Government, when the world government would come into existence, Mongolian (Chinese) forces would be patrolling from Southern California (where the communist Chinese COSCO (China Ocean Shipping Company) has a major presence in the port of Long Beach) into Mexico (where there is a major Chinese presence as well).

And in 1953, Ford Foundation president H. Rowan Gaither informed congressional Reece Committee research director Norman Dodd that they were under directives from the White House to "make every effort to so alter life in the United States as to make possible a comfortable merger with the Soviet Union." This is the synthesis desired by the PE.

The Cuban Missile Crisis of 1962 was portrayed as a great victory for President Kennedy against the Soviets, but it was a sham. The plan was that Soviet missiles in Cuba would be easily detected by the U.S., and the Soviets would agree to withdraw their missiles from Cuba in exchange for the U.S. withdrawing its missiles from Turkey and agreeing not to invade Cuba, which could then be used as a revolutionary training base for Latin America and Africa (e.g., Cuban troops went to Angola). In that same year, CFR member Lincoln Bloomfield prepared Study Memorandum No.7 for Secretary of State Dean Rusk (Rhodes scholar) in which Bloomfield described how a "world government" could come about, and then stated: "[But] if the communist dynamic was greatly abated, the

West might lose whatever incentive it has for world government." Again, we see how the dialectical synthesis is designed to work.

Another aspect of this process was revealed in James Simon Kunen's *The Strawberry Statement* (1968) regarding Students for a Democratic Society (SDS) convention:

> ... Men from Business International Roundtables ... tried to buy up a few radicals. Those men are the world's industrialists and they convene to decide how our lives are going to go. They're the left wing of the ruling class. They offered to finance our demonstrations in Chicago. We were also offered ESSO [Rockefeller] money. They want us to make a lot of radical commotion so they can look more in the center as they move more to the left.

This "move more to the left" by the power elite was important to open the door to trade and other relations with communist China, as David Rockefeller praised Chairman Mao's "accomplishments" in an article in the August 10, 1973, *New York Times.*

The PE had to bring communist China into the "community of nations" if their strategy of bringing about a world socialist government through linking regional economic arrangements was to work. The Far Eastern economic region would be linked to the Middle East, to Europe, to the Americas, and to Africa. Noncompliant people like Slobodan Milosevic in Yugoslavia and the Taliban in Afghanistan were stumbling blocks to fulfilling this plan, and therefore had to be removed.

In H. G. Wells' *Experiment in Autobiography,* he revealed that "the Open Conspiracy has to achieve itself in many ways, but the main battle before it is an educational battle." In the early 1980s at the U.S. Department of Education (DOE), I was assigned to brief a delegation from South Africa about DOE's programs and activities. It was about this same time (1984) U.S. Secretary of Education Terrel Bell and Utah State Superintendent Leland Burningham were exchanging letters about a plan to get outcome-based education (OBE) in all schools. The "Father of OBE" is William Spady, and his ultimate "transformational" OBE is designed to change students' values. On November 16, 1998, Spady arrived in South Africa to participate in two major educational conferences in Pretoria and Port Elizabeth.

The instability in Southern Africa, Israel, Palestine, Iraq, and elsewhere is all part of the dialectical process through which the PE plans to bring about a New World Order world socialist government. This New World Order will also have a spiritual component as represented in the Earth Charter, which I have explained elsewhere. Its authors, Mikhail Gorbachev and Maurice Strong (it was actually written by Steven Rockefeller), have both indicated the Earth Charter is like a new Ten Commandments, and it was presented to the U.N. not coincidentally at a conference in Johannesburg, South Africa. It will be a "common faith" just as H. G. Wells said in 1934. And this date (1934) is the same year John Dewey ("Father of Progressive Education" who wrote, "We are in for some kind of socialism") authored *A Common Faith*, in which he proposed "the surrender of the conception of the basic division to which supernatural Christianity is committed."

Previously, I referred to Cecil Rhodes' plan "to take the government of the whole world." In typical dialectical fashion, Rhodes' mentor, John Ruskin (who has a swastika on his grave), said both "I am a Tory [conservative] of the old school" and "I am myself a communist of the old school—reddest of the red." Rhodes' people networked dialectically with both Skull and Bones (mostly conservative) members and Fabian socialists (liberals).

When I was young, I was in touch with a number of world notables, and during my senior year in high school (1963–64), I was assigned to portray the famous historian Arnold Toynbee. He was an important member of Cecil Rhodes' Association of Helpers "to take the government of the whole world" (see reproduced

The Royal Institute of International Affairs

CHATHAM HOUSE

10 St James's Square, London SW1

Whitehall 2233

5 June 1964

Dear Mr Cuddy,

Thank you so much for your letter of May 14 with your speech-skit. I have enjoyed reading this. You have certainly done an immense amount of research into my ideas, and have reproduced these substantially right. I wonder whether I could have done as good a job on this, myself.

With thanks and best wishes,

Yours sincerely,

Arnold Toynbee

Mr Dennis L. Cuddy,
1018 Nichols Drive,
Raleigh,
North Carolina,
U.S.A.

letter from Toynbee above). From 1964 to 1968, I attended North Carolina State University where Allard Lowenstein was teaching, and I remember seeing and hearing him on occasion.

Previously, I mentioned that Lowenstein had worked in Africa, Spain, and Portugal for the CIA, which had been involved in university recruitment for some time. Lowenstein had received his B.A. degree from the University of North Carolina at Chapel Hill in 1949, and when I was attending graduate school there, one of my professors had been a CIA covert agent who encouraged me to go to CIA headquarters in Langley, Virginia, and another professor had been a Rhodes scholar in charge of the State Department's Middle East desk.

The ultimate goal of Cecil Rhodes and the PE was dialectically to synthesize Western capitalism and Eastern communism into a world socialist government. When Lowenstein was a student at UNC in the late 1940s, he was a member of a group called the Dialectic Senate. At this same time, the CIA was forming the

National Student Association (NSA), of which Lowenstein became president in 1950.

I also mentioned that in 1953, Ford Foundation president H. Rowan Gaither revealed that they were under directives from the White House to so alter life in the U.S. as to make possible a "comfortable merger" with the Soviet Union. Lowenstein would later work for the Ford Foundation (as well as the CIA). He also was in contact with quite a few Rhodes scholars, one of whom was Rick Stearns who was Bill Clinton's traveling companion at Oxford University as well as international vice president of the NSA in the mid-1960s.

I have emphasized the importance of South Africa in the dialectic, and now I shall look at Spain. Lowenstein and the CIA would present themselves as anti-communists who also opposed the right wing leadership in countries like South Africa and Spain (Francisco Franco). Note the dialectic—Lowenstein and the CIA would support the socialists as the alternative to the far left and far right political extremes. For years, Lowenstein had supported and networked with U.S. Socialist Party presidential candidate Norman Thomas. It is worth remembering here that during his 1948 presidential campaign, Thomas predicted: "The American people will never knowingly adopt socialism. But under the name of 'liberalism' they will adopt every fragment of the socialist program, until one day America will be a socialist nation, without knowing how it happened."

Lowenstein began making trips to Spain (for at least two decades) in 1958. And Richard Cummings in *The Pied Piper* (1984) indicated that Lowenstein "knew every Spanish opposition [to Franco] group and its leadership inside and out." In the early 1960s, he met with the Spanish Socialist Party (PSOE, Partido Socialista Obrero Espanol). And in 1964, a young Javier Solana while in college joined the PSOE.

The next year, Solana received a Fulbright scholarship to

begin a doctoral program in the U.S. The Fulbright scholarships were named for Rhodes scholar Bill Clinton's political mentor, U.S. Senator J. William Fulbright of Arkansas. In mid-April 1964, Lowenstein was invited along with President and Mrs. Lyndon Johnson to be dinner guests at the home of Sen. Fulbright. And that same year, Sen. Fulbright authored *Old Myths and New Realities*, announcing that "the concept of national sovereignty has become in our time a principle of international anarchy. ... The sovereign nation can no longer serve as the ultimate unit of personal loyalty and responsibility." As an example of how the dialectic works, while Rhodes scholar Sen. Fulbright was a "dove" on the Vietnam War, Rhodes scholar Secretary of State Dean Rusk was a "hawk." Cecil Rhodes' plan for world government was always the goal, though, and in March 1994, a World Affairs Council chapter awarded Dean Rusk its "World Citizen Award."

After receiving the Ph.D. from the University of Virginia in 1968, and then teaching there as an assistant professor until 1971, Solana returned to Madrid to teach and become active again in Spanish politics in the early 1970s. In a phone interview July 14, 2006, Richard Cummings told me that Lowenstein and Solana probably did know each other.

During this time, Rhodes scholar Richard Gardner in the April 1974 edition of the Council on Foreign Relation's (CFR's) *Foreign Affairs* wrote that "an end run around national sovereignty, eroding it piece by piece, will accomplish much more than the old-fashioned frontal assault." Gardner in the article went on to explain how GATT (including the World Trade Organization) would be part of this process.

The next year (1975), Spanish ruler Francisco Franco died, and in 1977 Solana was elected to the Spanish parliament and opposed U.S. military bases in Spain. In 1982, just before the PSOE came to power, Spain joined NATO with Solana in opposition to that decision. However, later that same year, after the PSOE came to power, Solana was appointed Minister for Culture and reversed his position. According to *Encyclopaedia Britannica*, "in 1986 he was pivotal in organizing a referendum to endorse Spain's membership in NATO." At this point, it is worth remembering that under the dialectic, the CIA befriended (funded) socialists in Spain to control them or at least make them less radical.

Solana in 1988 was appointed Minister for Education and Science, and became Minister for Foreign Affairs in 1992. This was the same year Bill Clinton ran for the presidency, and his advisor on U.N. matters was fellow Rhodes scholar Richard Gardner.

After Clinton's election, he would appoint his Rhodes scholar roommate, Strobe Talbott, to the State Department where he eventually became the number two person. During the presidential campaign, Talbott had written in *Time* magazine (July 20, 1992) that "perhaps national sovereignty wasn't such a great idea after all. ... But it has taken the events in our own wondrous and terrible century to clinch the case for world government."

The number one man in the State Department, CFR member Warren Christopher, during his January 13, 1993, Senate confirmation hearing, discussed with Sen. Joseph Biden the possibility of NATO becoming a peacekeeping surrogate for the U.N. "to foster the creation of a new world order." Thus, the people in charge of NATO politically and militarily would be of critical importance.

It was no surprise, therefore, that President Clinton appointed fellow Rhodes scholar Gen. Wesley Clark to be military head of NATO. However, after Javier Solana became the political head of NATO on December 5, 1995, *Encyclopaedia Britannica* stated, "He was somewhat unexpectedly chosen." After all, Solana only occupied a ministerial position in Spain. How was he selected over all other candidates?

The key lies in President Clinton's appointment of Richard Gardner as U.S. ambassador to Spain. Gardner and his fellow Rhodes scholars Clinton and Talbott sealed the "cooperative"

Solana's appointment as political head of NATO. I use the word "cooperative" because while Solana only approved of Spain's membership in NATO in the 1980s provided Spain's armed forces didn't participate in military operations, in the late 1990s as NATO Secretary-General he sent sixty thousand troops from thirty countries into Bosnia and Herzegovina (just as Clinton, Talbott, and Gardner desired).

Solana would go on to become on June 29, 2004, the European Union's first Minister for Foreign Affairs, and from 1999 to 2009, he was Secretary-General of the Council of the European Union. He has been one of the most powerful men in the world, and strategically placed by the dialectic to facilitate the New World Order, Cecil Rhodes' plan "to take the government of the whole world."

Not only are people like Solana useful to the PE in this regard, but so are U.S. Presidents like Bill Clinton and George W. Bush (Skull and Bones member, as were his father and grandfather). The dialectic uses left and right, liberal and conservative. In this regard, if you look at the White House website, you will see in the Oval Office a carpet with the Great Seal of the United States (just like on the one dollar bill), and the eagle is looking left. However, if you look at the emblem on the front of the president's desk, the eagle is looking right! Is this dialectical symbolism?

As I have explained before, the PE's plan is to link regional economic arrangements to form a world socialist government. Some of the world's people are getting wise to this, and when U.S. trade negotiators arrived in Seoul, South Korea, on July 9, 2006, to discuss a "free-trade agreement," they had to have government bodyguards because of the protesters there.

The PE wants Korea (South and North) to become part of a larger Asian-Pacific regional economic arrangement, which can then be linked to NAFTA, the European Economic Community (European Union), Africa, etc. The dialectic uses a certain amount of chaos (e.g., uncontrolled borders, violent confrontations, etc.)

to cause the people to accept transnational "agreements" (not treaties, which would have to be ratified by the U.S. Senate). The South Koreans probably will be "persuaded" that part of their security against the current aggressive gestures (missile launches) by North Korea will depend upon their willingness to accept a "free-trade agreement," which might then be offered to North Korea as well.

In the Middle East, there is chaos between Israelis and Palestinians. The PE hopes to weary these people, and then offer the "carrot" of the Middle East Free Trade Area (MEFTA), which then can be linked with other regions. President George W. Bush indicated that he wanted all nations of the Middle East under one regional economic authority by 2013. There is a lobbying group (including Exxon, Mobil, Bechtel, and Halliburton) called the U.S.-MEFTA Coalition promoting an economic arrangement between the two regions. Roxane Premont in her NewsWithViews article, "Sacrificing America for Global Trade" (July 8, 2006), concluded that if this arrangement came about, "it would be entirely plausible for a company like Dubai Ports to sue the United States government and win in court," because local businesses cannot be favored over foreign companies.

How do Solana and Spain fit in all this? Javier Solana arranged a treaty of association (including security, trade, etc.) between the European Union and Israel, which was signed November 20, 1995, and officially ratified June 1, 2000. According to Herb Keinon's June 6, 2006, article in *The Jerusalem Post,* on June 5, 2006, Javier Solana met in Israel with officials there, telling them he "remained firm on the need for the Hamas-PA [Palestinian Authority] government to meet these criteria before gaining international legitimacy: recognizing Israel, renouncing terrorism and accepting previous agreements."

Relevant to Spain, there was a plan to build a massive Trans-America highway splitting the U.S. in half and running from Mexico to Canada, facilitating a North American region with the

"Amero" as a new currency. The first stage was the TransTexas Corridor, which would be built by Zachry Construction Company of Texas (George Bush's home state) and managed by CINTRA, a Madrid, Spain, company which already manages toll highways around the world, including some in the U.S. Is it possible that Javier Solana of Madrid, Spain, had a hand in that?

## The Power Elite's Planned Dialectical "Crisis"

Previously, I have explained that the PE uses a dialectical process in order to achieve its objectives, and I thought it would be helpful to explain how this has been used giving a specific historical event: the Cuban missile crisis. Most people believe the Soviets tried to place offensive nuclear missiles in Cuba, and they only backed down when President Kennedy discovered what they had done and forced them to remove the missiles. What REALLY was going on was a dialectical thesis of missile placement, followed by a PLANNED discovery (antithesis), and a synthesis of both the Soviets and the U.S. withdrawing missiles from near each other's nation, along with a U.S. guarantee not to invade Cuba. This was the dialectical goal all along, so that Cuba could be used as a revolutionary training base for Central America and Africa. The following is a detailed explanation:

At the conclusion of the 1962 Cuban missile crisis between the United States and the Soviet Union, the withdrawal by the U.S.S.R. of offensive missiles from Cuba was heralded as a great victory for President Kennedy. But in exchange for this withdrawal, the president guaranteed the safety of Castro's Cuba from additional invasion attempts from the United States. What a few of us have asked since that time is, what if the guarantee was what the Soviets expected all along?

In January 1989, top-level Soviet, American, and Cuban officials who had been involved in the missile crisis held a two-day conference in Moscow in which Sergei Khrushchev, son of the late Soviet leader Nikita Khrushchev, admitted, "Even in event of an American invasion or air strike, Soviet officials in Cuba had no orders to use the missiles."

That only stands to reason, because what sense would it have made for the U.S.S.R. to risk nuclear confrontation with the United States just to obtain offensive missiles in Cuba, ninety miles from the American mainland, when nuclear-armed Soviet submarines would come even closer to our eastern, southern and western coasts? Would it not have made more sense for the Soviet presidium to conclude that because the United States was militarily superior, there was no way to win a nuclear fight?

However, since American missiles were still in Turkey (despite earlier orders by the president to remove them), this gave the Soviets an excuse to place missiles in Cuba. Of course, this would be followed by an American objection to their presence, and the U.S.S.R. could then appear conciliatory by offering to remove the missiles in exchange for the removal of ours from Turkey, along with a guarantee for the safety of Castro's Cuba from American intervention.

But what evidence is there that the Soviets expected an eventual withdrawal of missiles from Cuba in exchange for the safety guarantee? The evidence is as follows:

» In his excellent work, *Essence of Decision,* Graham Allison stated: "Missile deployment and evidence of Soviet actions toward détente poses an apparent contradiction."
» The Soviets knew of Cuban U-2 flights.
» The missiles were left uncamouflaged.
» The Soviets did not coordinate installation of the medium-range ballistic missiles with the completion of the surface-to-air missile covers.

» The Soviet Union had never before placed missiles in any nation beyond its borders, not even in its satellites in East Europe.

» Cuba hypothetically could eventually expel the Soviet technicians (as Anwar Sadat later did in Egypt) and do whatever it pleased with the missiles— perhaps take actions that would result in World War III (a situation not to be encouraged by the U.S.S.R.) or perhaps allow American acquisition of the missiles if friendly relations were re-established between Cuba and the United States.

» The United States had already attempted one invasion and would certainly succeed with a second one if it so chose.

» The Soviets desired to avert a nuclear confrontation, yet wanted to use Cuba as a training ground for Latin American revolutionaries.

» And perhaps the best argument for this hypothesis is the post facto one of recent history—the missiles were removed in exchange for the safety guarantee, and Cuba has been used for the training of revolutionaries.

Some have objected that the expectation of missile removal does not square with the secretive Soviet method of transporting the missiles to Cuba and from the docks there to their ultimate launch sites. But I would maintain that this behavior squares exactly. What good would it have done for the Soviets to announce that they were going to send missiles to Cuba, or that the missiles were on the boats either on the way to Cuba or at the dock there? What concessions from the United States could have been gained?

The United States could have more effectively quarantined Cuba or made surgical air strikes more confidently, among other alternatives. With the missiles already in Cuba, and at their sites, on the other hand, a quarantine would not have removed the missiles there, and even surgical air strikes would have hit civilians and placed the U.S. in an unfavorable light in world affairs, especially in Latin America.

In case you think the U.S. was oblivious to Castro being a communist in the 1950s, the American ambassador to Cuba at the time, Earl E. T. Smith, in his *The Fourth Floor* (1962) related that he informed U.S. officials such was the case. And in Dr. Stan Monteith's 1980 interview with the ambassador (see Radio Liberty's video "The World Revolution" [https://www.youtube.com/watch?v=ACO7BtR9lXc]), the latter says the U.S. helped bring Castro to power anyway. Also, power elite member David Rockefeller's daughter is a good friend of Castro, as is European Union power elite member Javier Solana, who was brought to power by Rhodes scholars Bill Clinton, Strobe Talbott, and Richard Gardner.

And remember, the so-called Cuban Missile Crisis occurred about seven months after CFR member Lincoln Bloomfield's March 10, 1962, study Memorandum No. 7 from the State Department (headed by Rhodes scholar Dean Rusk) regarding how a "world government" would come about. He stated: "If the communist dynamic was greatly abated, the West might lose whatever incentive it has for world government."

This is how the PE works. And that the U.S. is controlled by the PE is obvious. Why else would the U.S. overthrow Saddam, who was replaced by a Muslim-controlled government, which allows Christians to be constantly persecuted? This is right after the U.S. intervened in the Balkans because Kosovo Muslims were being persecuted; and then the U.S. supported Kosovo independence even though it would become a breeding ground for the Al Qaeda, which is even killing U.S. soldiers today! Logically, it doesn't make sense. But the PE wants conflict (dialectical thesis versus antithesis) so that it can bring its (New World) Order (synthesis) out of it in the form of a world socialist government with a new world religion (common faith), with which all can agree (that would eliminate Jesus as Savior, because some disagree).

## Dialectics, Rockefellers, and Population Control

As I have mentioned many times before, the PE's favorite means of controlling people is the dialectical process. This often involves creating a "threat" to a particular population. For example, the terrorist threat after 9/11 caused Americans to be willing to give up certain of their freedoms which they had been unwilling to give up before 9/11.

I advise people to look at any incident not just in terms of its face value, but also in terms of how it might fit into the PE's dialectical process. For example, the CIA in 2003 learned from captured Al Qaeda operatives about their planned "American Hiroshima" to explode seven nuclear devices in American cities. Paul Williams, author of *The Al Qaeda Connection,* has explained that several of these devices were developed, sent to Mexico, and slipped into the U.S. Why haven't they been used? They would have if one takes this at face value, because Al Qaeda wouldn't wait for the weapons to degrade or be discovered. They would not have been used, however, if the operation is really controlled by people above these radical Islamic frontmen!

If Osama bin Laden could find nineteen terrorists willing to kill themselves for the cause, do you really think that in the last ten years before his death he couldn't find any others willing to bring the U.S. economy to a halt by simple terrorist acts nationwide against our rail, food, etc., systems without having to kill themselves in the process? Of course, he could find many such people. But they haven't attacked, have they? Ask yourself, "Why haven't they?" Could it be because they are controlled by those above Al Qaeda?

Another example of the dialectical process used to threaten a particular population can be seen in the leader of Iran making threats against Israel. A tendency of most people is to see this as only that—a radical Muslim's anger toward Israel. But if you look at it as part of a dialectical process, it becomes quite different.

Many times before, I have quoted Lincoln Bloomfield's 1961 study for the U.S. State Department as stating that if the communist dynamic/threat were greatly abated, the West would lose whatever incentive it has for world government. In case you think this is just a theory, remember what happened to Hungary. By October 28, 1956, Hungarian patriots had driven the Soviets away, but the U.S. State Department then sent a cable to Yugoslavian dictator Tito saying "the government of the United States does not look with favor upon governments unfriendly to the Soviet Union on the borders of the Soviet Union." This was a green light for the Soviets to crush the Hungarians, thus leaving the communist dynamic/threat alive and well.

Now apply this princple to Iran and Israel. If the radical Islamic (Iranian) threat were greatly abated, Israel would have less incentive to become part of a world government. Just as the American population is being manipulated/controlled, so are the Israelis.

You might ask why Isreal doesn't simply bomb Iranian nuclear facilities, but another part of the dialectical process involves "pressure." Israel, like every other nation, must worry about the consequences of any action, and if it bombed Iran, what would be the responses of Muslims, the U.S., Russia, China, etc., not just militarily but also economically in terms of foreign aid, investments, and the world's oil supply?

One of the families connected to the PE is the Rockefeller family, as former Congressman William Dannemeyer has recounted that David Rockefeller told him that some men are born to rule, but most men are born to be ruled. Therefore, it would be useful to look at a chronology regarding the Rockefellers and population control:

» **August 1904.** *Everybody's Magazine* publishes Thomas Lawson's "Frenzied Finance," in which he reveals that Standard Oil

(Rockefeller) agents are "in every hamlet in the country," and that once someone is within their network, "punishment for disloyalty is sure and terrible, and in no corner of the earth can he escape it."

» **1910.** The Eugenics Record Office is established at Cold Spring Harbor in New York. It is funded by the Carnegie Institute, and will receive funding from the Rockefeller Foundation which will be founded in 1913. The Rockefeller Foundation also will fund Nazi Dr. Ernst Rudin's eugenics research at the Kaiser Wilhelm Brain Research Institute in Berlin. At the Third International Congress on Eugenics held in New York in 1932, Rudin will be unanimously elected president of the International Federation of Eugenic Societies. Rudin and other Nazis will be transported to the Congress on George Herbert Walker's and Prescott Bush's Hamburg-Amerika Lines.

» **1911.** John D. Rockefeller, Jr., forms the Bureau of Social Hygiene, and in 1913 the Rockefeller Foundation will help organize and fund the American Social Hygiene Association "for reconsideration of public attitudes toward prostitution." Via the National Research Council, the Rockefeller Foundation's Medical Division for many years will fund the horrible sex research of Alfred Kinsey. In the early 1900s, Rockefeller introduces Margaret Sanger to the monied elite who help her form the Birth Control League that will become Planned Parenthood. She eugenically advocates limiting "dysgenic stocks" such as blacks, Hispanics, American Indians and Catholics, as well as "slum dwellers" such as Jewish immigrants.

» **August 1912.** Frederick Gates, head of the Rockefeller General Education Board (GEB, founded in 1902), writes in *The World's Work* that "in our dream we have limitless resources, and the [rural] people yield themselves with perfect docility to our molding hand."

» **March 27, 1922.** *The New York Times* reports that New York

City mayor John Hylan said: "One of my first acts as mayor was to pitch out, bag and baggage, from the educational system of our city the Rockefeller agents" who supported "the kind of education the coolies receive in China."

» **April 11, 1933.** Rockefeller Foundation president Max Mason assures trustees that in their program, "the Social Sciences will concern themselves with the rationalization of social control, ... the control of human behavior."

» **Fall 1937.** Rockefeller Foundation gives a grant to Princeton University to study the influence of radio on different groups, and a grant by the GEB will be made to study how the broadcast of *The War of the Worlds* fit into the Princeton Project.

» **1937.** Robert Havighurst becomes director of the GEB and suggests the "global servant" concept and educating youth for some form of world citizenship.

» **1939.** Rockefeller Foundation organizes a series of secret seminars involving communications scholars with the aim of manipulating Americans to accept involvement in World War II. This is part of a larger effort before 1945 whereby the Rockefeller Foundation underwrites Harold Laswell and Walter Lippmann, who advocated a world in which elites ruled by manipulating mass sentiment.

» **March 27, 1942.** Senator Harry Truman refers to the Standard Oil (Rockefeller) dealings with the Nazis as "approaching treason."

» **1945.** Rockefeller Foundation medical director Alan Gregg begins search for an institution that will see if wartime psychology could be relevant for civilian society. Regarding this, the foundation will fund the Tavistock Institute of Human Relations.

» **1950–51.** Rockefeller Foundation chairman John Foster Dulles takes John D. Rockefeller III on a tour of Third World countries stressing the need eugenically to control the growth of non-white populations.

» **1952.** John D. Rockefeller III and John Foster Dulles found the Population Council to fund population control measures.

» **1959.** Rockefeller Brothers Fund (for whom a young Henry Kissinger has worked) publishes *The Mid-Century Challenge To U.S. Foreign Policy,* in which one reads: "We cannot escape, and indeed should welcome, the task which history has imposed on us. This is the task of helping to shape a new world order in all its dimensions—spiritual, economic, political, social."

» **September 1961.** Former Rockefeller Foundation president Dean Rusk (Rhodes scholar) as secretary of state publishes "Freedom From War" detailing a three-stage disarmament plan, including "the disbanding of all national armies ... other than those required to preserve internal order and for contributions to the United Nations Peace Force."

» **1968.** James Simon Kunen's *The Strawberry Statement* is published and includes a report from a meeting of the radical Students for a Democratic Society, which indicated they "were offered ESSO [Rockefeller] money to make a lot of radical commotion so they [left wing of ruling class] can look more in the center as they move more to the left."

» **March 11, 1969.** Vice president of Planned Parenthood-World Population Frederick Jaffe's "Activities Relevant to the Study of Population Policy for the U.S." is printed containing a memo to Population Council president Bernard Berelson. It includes examples of proposed measures to reduce U.S. fertility, such as (a) encourage increased homosexuality, (b) fertility control agents in water supply, (c) encourage women to work, (d) abortion and sterilization on demand, and (e) make contraception truly available and accessible to all.

» **March 20, 1969.** Dr. Lawrence Dunegan attends a meeting of pediatric physicians in Pittsburgh where the speaker is Dr. Richard Day, national medical director of Planned Parenthood (funded by the Rockefeller Foundation) from 1965–68. Dr. Dunegan recounts that Dr. Day said that in the future there will be hard-to-cure diseases created, and that cures for nearly all cancers had been developed but were being hidden at the Rockefeller Institute so that populations would not increase.

» **July 1, 1970.** Senate Appropriations hearings are held for the Department of Defense and refer to eminent biologists who believe that within five to ten years it would be possible to produce a synthetic biological agent (infective micro-organism), an agent that does not naturally exist and for which no natural immunity could have been acquired. Tentative plans to initiate a program to develop such an agent were discussed by the National Research Council (remember it was via the National Research Council that the Rockefeller Foundation funded Alfred Kinsey's research). Hearings in the British House of Commons from April 8 to May 13, 1987, regarding AIDS will include the following:

> Every biological scientist who has dispassionately studied the virus and the epidemic knows that the origins of the virus could lie in the developments of modern biology. ... Some who know perfectly well what has happened are deliberately fudging scientific data to keep the heat off them and fellow members of their molecular biological "club."

» **1970.** David Rockefeller becomes chairman of the Council on Foreign Relations (CFR) until 1985. During this time, Rhodes scholar Richard Gardner will write "The Hard Road to World Order" in the CFR's *Foreign Affairs* (April 1974), in which he will advocate that "an end run around national sovereignty, eroding it piece-by-piece, will accomplish much more than the old-fashioned frontal assault."

» **March 7, 1972.** The Rockefeller Commission on Population issues a report advocating population control, stating that further growth of the American population could cause economic problems, and that "in any case, no generation needs to know the ultimate goal or the final means, only the direction to which they will be found." In other words, they will control population, but they're not going to tell us how!

» **August 10, 1973.** *The New York Times* publishes an article by David Rockefeller praising "the social experiment in China under Chairman Mao's leadership," despite the fact that tens of millions of innocent people have been slaughtered by the communist dictatorship there.

» **1973.** The Trilateral Commission is begun by David Rockefeller and will issue a report stating that "population planning should be an integral part of social and economic development."

» **1973.** George H. W. Bush praises the Population Crisis Committee (PCC) for having played a "major role in assisting government policy makers and in mobilizing United States' response to the world population challenge." The PCC was founded by Gen. William Draper, Jr. (vice-chairman of Planned Parenthood), and is largely funded by the Rockefeller Foundation.

» **1973.** *The Second American Revolution* by John D. Rockefeller III is published and applauds sexual liberation and the "humanistic revolution" while disparaging "old-fashioned nationalism."

» **1974.** CFR chairman David Rockefeller (and other globalists) encourage David R. Young to form in early 1975 Oxford Analytica, which will be the first private-sector, overt, global intelligence network. Among its clients will be the U.N., NATO, the World Bank, Chase Manhattan Bank, Bechtel, ChevronTexaco, Shell Oil, IBM, etc. Among its international advisory board will be Rhodes scholar and former U.S. senator Bill Bradley as well as James O'Toole who is Mortimer J. Adler Senior Fellow at The Aspen Institute. And among its members will be Rick Warren, mega-church pastor and author of *The Purpose Driven Life,* who is also a member of the CFR.

» **1974.** Toward the end of the year, John D. Rockefeller III addresses delegates to the Population Tribune in Bucharest, Rumania, and declares that "population planning must be a fundamental and integral part of any modern development program, recognized as such by national leadership and supported fully."

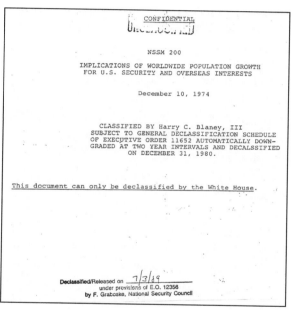

» **December 10, 1974.** The National Security Council's NSSM 200, "Implications of Worldwide Population Growth for U.S. Security and Overseas Interests," is marked "classified" and "confidential." It is proposed by Secretary of State Henry Kissinger (formerly with the Rockefeller Brothers Fund) and will be given final approval by national security advisor Brent Scowcroft. The document states:

> ... if future numbers are to be kept within reasonable bounds, it is urgent that measures to reduce fertility be started and made

effective in the 1970s and 1980s. ... [Financial] assistance will be given to other countries, considering such factors as population growth. ... Food and agricultural assistance is vital for any population sensitive development strategy. ... Allocation of scarce resources should take account of what steps a country is taking in population control. ... There is an alternative view that mandatory programs may be needed. ...

» **1975.** Rockefeller Foundation president John Knowles in the annual report states:

> The web of interdependence is tightening. We are one world and there will be one future—for better or for worse—for us all. Central to a new ethic of making less more is controlled economic growth which conserves scarce resources, provides equitable distribution of income and wealth. ... It is also necessary to control fertility rates at the replacement level and to achieve zero population growth as rapidly as possible.

» **November 1977.** The Soviet *New Times* reports that David Rockefeller just sent a message to Kremlin leaders saying: "My congratulations on the occasion of the 60th anniversary of the October Revolution." This is despite the fact that the Soviets have killed tens of millions of innocent people.

» **December 1980.** Archbishop Peter Proeku Dery of Ghana reveals that

> ... the World Bank denied loans to Ghana until my country agreed to institute a nationwide contraception and family planning policy. There was also pressure to legalize abortion, although the Church and the people have so far been able to prevent this. For how long, I don't know. The World Bank's attitude shows a total disregard for the beliefs of the people of the Third World.

Some years later, Kofi Annan of Ghana will receive the approval of the PE to become U.N. Secretary-General, and he will do nothing to stop the slaughter of hundreds of thousands of Rwandans.

» **April 19, 1985.** Jim Grob of "The Rockefeller Project" writes a memo on Seattle Public Schools stationery, and it cautions that "the term 'global education' is an extreme, political hot potato at this time" with "right-wing Christian groups" opposing its use, and that instead of using the term "global education," district personnel should note that a "temporarily safe term is multicultural/international curriculum development."

» **1986.** Rockefeller Foundation gives grants of $6.3 million to various population programs. Rev. Theodore Hesburgh, a Catholic priest and president of the University of Notre Dame, has served as chairman of the foundation's board of trustees from 1977 to 1982.

» **1986.** William Henry Draper III (Skull and Bones member) becomes head of the U.N. Development Program (UNDP), a position for which he was recommended by Vice President George H. W. Bush (Skull and Bones member). He will hold this position until 1993 when he will become vice-chairman of Population Action International. The UNDP acts as an adjunct of the World Bank and promotes population reduction in Third World countries. It is worth remembering here that the Skull and Bones secret society to which Draper and Bush belong requires its members to take a secret oath and has secret proceedings. Relevant to this, President John F. Kennedy in an April 27, 1961, speech at the Waldorf Astoria declared: "The very word 'secrecy' is repugnant to a free and open society; and we are as a people inherently and historically opposed to secret societies, to secret oaths and to secret proceedings."

» **January 1, 1987.** On William F. Buckley, Jr.'s television program "Crossfire," Faye Wattleton (president of Planned Parenthood, which has been funded by the Rockefeller Foundation) acknowledges: "We have received contributions from people who want to support us because they want ... all black women to stop having children." Think about why an organization would accept such funds given for such a purpose, rather than refusing such contributions for that purpose. Remember Planned Parenthood founder Margaret Sanger's "Negro Project" proposal stated: "The mass of Negroes, particularly in the South, still breed carelessly and disastrously ... [and is] from that portion of the population least intelligent and fit." In October 1939, Sanger wrote a letter to Procter & Gamble heir Clarence Gamble relating how they would deal with such a "problem." The next month (November 1939), Sanger's *Birth Control Review* commended the Nazi birth control program, saying that "the German program has been much more carefully worked out [than the Italian program]. The need for quality as well as quantity is recognized." In the April 1933 *Birth Control Review* was an article, "Eugenic Sterilization: An Urgent Need," by Nazi Dr. Ernst Rudin (funded by the Rockefeller Foundation).

» **1987.** Rockefeller Foundation funds in part the publication of Arthur Miller's *The Secret Constitution and the Need for Constitutional Change,* in which one reads Miller's assertion that

> ... a pervasive system of thought control exists in the United States. ... The citizenry is indoctrinated by employment of the mass media and the system of public education. ... People are told what to think about. ... The old order is crumbling. ... Nationalism should be seen as a dangerous social disease. ... A new vision is required to plan and manage the future, a global vision that will transcend national boundaries and eliminate the poison of nationalistic 'solutions.' ... A new Constitution is necessary. ... Americans really have no choice, for constitutional alteration will come whether or not it is liked or planned for.

... Ours is the age of the planned society. ... No other way is possible.

» **February 10, 1988.** Sidney Blumenthal in *The Washington Post* quotes David Rockefeller as claiming: "He's [George H. W. Bush] one of us ['The Establishment']. ... If Bush were President, he would be in a better position than anyone else to pull together the people in the country who believe that we are in fact living in one world and have to act that way."

» **January 1991.** William Henry Draper III gives a speech in Washington, DC, revealing that population reduction is a key component of President Bush's "new world order."

» **November 11, 1992.** National Center on Education and the Economy (NCEE) president Marc Tucker writes a letter to NCEE board member Hillary Clinton saying he has recently been in the office of NCEE board member David Rockefeller, Jr., who was celebrating Bill Clinton's election as president of the U.S. Tucker explains how this will give them a chance to implement their plan to integrate education into a human resources development system "that literally extends from cradle to grave and is the same system for everyone —young and old, poor and rich. ... Radical changes in attitudes, values and beliefs are required to move any combination of these agendas. ... "

» **July 1, 1995.** Rockefeller Foundation trustee (1979–1985) James Wolfensohn becomes president of the World Bank until May 31, 2005. The World Bank has funded population control efforts around the world, and Wolfensohn was a trustee of Rockefeller's Population Council from 1977 to 1984.

» **1997.** Rockefeller Foundation gives $2 million to Hua Lian Pharmaceutical in Shanghai to upgrade its factory, which has been for years producing the RU-486 abortion drug as a key ingredient in China's population control strategy. On October

12, 2000, *The Washington Post* will indicate this factory will produce RU-486 for the U.S.

» **1998.** *Threshold 2000: Critical Issues and Spiritual Values for a Global Age* is published by the Millennium Institute, founded in 1993 by its executive director Gerald O. Barney, formerly head of the Rockefeller Brothers Fund National Program. The institute has been funded by the Rockefeller Foundation and Rockefeller Brothers Fund, among others. Barney and two others wrote *Threshold 2000*, in which one reads:

> The premise of "sovereignty" underlying modern nation-states is false. … [Nations] are all interdependent. … Nation-states must change radically. … Within a few decades, the fallacious notion of sovereignty must disappear and be replaced with an understanding that "nations" (or whatever name we give to the institutions that replace nation-states) are all intimately interconnected with each other and with Earth.

Concerning the earth's population, Barney *et al.* say that a rapid drop in human fertility is needed, and for that to occur, "it will be necessary to change the religious, social, economic, and legal factors that shape couples' decisions on the number of children they have." And he advises humans to work together to "create the religious, social, and economic conditions necessary to stop the growth of human population. … "

» **2002.** David Rockefeller in his *Memoirs* reveals:

> Some even believe we [Rockefeller family] are part of a secret cabal working against the best interests of the United States, characterizing my family and me as "internationalists" and of conspiring with others around the world to build a more integrated global political and economic structure—one world, if you will. If that's the charge, I stand guilty, and I am proud of it.

Some people believe this revelation was a slip-up by Rockefeller, but I doubt it. I think it was a psychological probe (e.g., the American people psychologically conditioned not to stop the killing of Terri Schiavo) the power elite periodically performs to see what the public is willing to accept or overlook, and apparently this was successful. Have you seen any media reports about Rockefeller's remark, and have you seen any large number of the public expressing their shock and outrage over it?

» **March 6, 2004.** *Weekly Trust* of Nigeria publishes an interview with Dr. Haruna Kaita who reports that lab tests show the oral polio vaccines given to children contained harmful and toxic contaminants, some with a direct effect upon human reproductive systems (the result being limiting population growth). Dr. Kaita then revealed: "These manufacturers or promoters of these harmful things have a secret agenda." Tetanus vaccines given three to five times a year to Philippine women have been shown to contain antifertility agents, thereby also limiting population growth.

Chapter 8

# Other Power Elite Techniques

## A Variety of Techniques and Mechanisms

Bobby Jindal, son of immigrants from India, was recently elected governor of Louisiana not long ago. He's a Rhodes scholar. Why would anyone want a scholarship named for a man who paid blacks very little to extricate under awful conditions gold and diamonds for him? And remember Cecil Rhodes' plan for world government.

Also remember in H. G. Wells' 1933 book, *The Shape of Things To Come,* he said the future world government would come out of a conference in Basra, Iraq! Why else do you think the PE has the U.S. involved in a country where, according to Terry McCarthy of ABC News on March 14, 2007, over half of all Iraqis think it's all right to attack U.S. soldiers? Logically, Americans wouldn't fight for a people who want to kill them, so there has to be another agenda at work.

Historically, the PE's influence goes back to the founding of our nation. On page 492 of volume 1 of *The Revolutionary Diplomatic Correspondence of the United States,* compiled by Dr. Francis Wharton and promulgated on August 13, 1888, by both houses of Congress, one reads:

No sovereign in Europe was watched with greater interest or regard as wielding a more supreme authority than was [Benjamin] Franklin by English politicians as the [American Revolutionary] war progressed. ... As far as his personal relations, his past is to be considered. He undoubtedly had been much flattered in France, and pleasantly accepted the courtesies which were part of this flattery. But this flattery, it must be remembered, came not from the government but rather from philosophical illuminati. ...

Today, two of the PE's control mechanisms are "hype," as George Orwell in *1984* warned about "quickening the tempo of human life," and numbing people to violence. For example, the Macy's Thanksgiving Day parade on November 22, 2007, featured one hyped performing group after another yelling or screaming so-called music and frenetically jerking themselves inside-out in so-called dance.

The Philadelphia parade was no better, as the apparently violence-numbed TV hosts said we're now "celebrating" a real historical pirate, Sam Bellamy, as a musical group in pirate dress followed cheerfully singing, "Are you ready to party?" Understand—this isn't some fictional Long John Silver or Disney character. They were "celebrating" a real pirate who captured over five hundred ships, brutally attacking people, cutting their bodies open with his sword, and stealing everything his victims owned! The people of Philadelphia were actually standing there smiling and applauding this "celebration." This demonstrates just how sick the conditioned American public has become.

People's mental numbness has also been applied to spiritual issues as well. Not very long ago, religious leader Pat Robertson publicly endorsed Rudolph Giuliani for president, despite the anti-biblical positions of Giuliani on issues such as abortion and homosexuality, in addition to Giuliani's divorces plus his anti-Second

Amendment positions. Giuliani supposedly is a Catholic, and Catholic as well as Episcopal religious leaders have proclaimed Jesus isn't the only way to Heaven. One might therefore ask them why anyone should become a Catholic or Episcopalian if one can be a good Hindu, or whatever, and still go to Heaven? While that question might not phase them, if you then ask them why any-one should contribute financially to them rather than to Hindus, etc., because of their attitude about Christ, that might just get their attention so that they'll wake up to the truth of salvation only through Jesus.

Other mechanisms that can be used by the power elite are sound and tracking devices. American Technologies-patented HyperSound can "beam" sounds to specific people that only those individuals can hear. The U.S. Air Force has also experimented with similar microwave devices which they consider possible psy-chological warfare tools. DARPA (Defense Advanced Research Projects Agency) has a Sonic Projector which can perform similar functions.

In terms of tracking people, about sixteen years ago, Brazil began obligating the implantation of the National System of Auto-matic Identification of Vehicles that is capable of identifying vehi-cles in the Brazilian fleet. Identification can be made via electronic plates and integrated system antennas. Thus, vehicles can be used to track people's movements and specific locations.

Lastly, the PE uses government leaders to move us toward their goal of a world socialist government. For example, if Hillary Clin-ton becomes president, she has been on a Rhodes scholar selection committee, and her husband is a Rhodes scholar. Her healthcare plan (HillaryCare) has been described as socialistic (perhaps she first could have a mental health exam of the people of Philadelphia who "celebrated" a real cutthroat pirate). And on June 29, 2004, she said, "We're going to take things from you on behalf of the common good." Then, on June 4, 2007, she announced, "I certainly think the free market has failed." Both remarks were cheered by socialists, and cemented her approval by the PE.

## If War Had Not Come in Fierce and Exaggerated Form

A movie, *Valkyrie,* with Tom Cruise, was released in 2008, and in an interview Cruise said he was surprised by the openness of Col. Claus von Stauffenberg (the character Cruise plays) in discussing his plot to kill Hitler in 1944. What Cruise and most people don't understand is that Hitler's ability to begin and wage WWII were facilitated by the PE!

From the American perspective, the PE's use of wars goes back over two hundred years. The PE was concerned that the young American republic was too independent of their control. I've mentioned in previous columns Philip Freneau's article in *American Museum* in 1792 describing how the PE would regain control of the U.S., and their use of a war and its predetermined outcome. I've also already described how the Civil War was designed to create a gulf empire, splitting the South from the rest of the U.S.

On February 5, 1891, Cecil Rhodes as a member of the PE began his secret Society of the Elect after writing to his close friend W. T. Stead that his (Rhodes') idea would "ultimately lead to the cessation of all wars. ... The only thing feasible to carry this idea out is a secret one [society] gradually absorbing the wealth of the world to be devoted to such an object. ... Fancy the charm to young America ... to share in a scheme to take the government of the whole world!" Among Rhodes' Association of Helpers (AH) were two Germans, Helmuth James von Moltke and Adam von Trott zu Solz. The AH formed Round Table groups, out of which would come the Council on Foreign Relations (CFR), largely funded by J. P. Morgan interests.

World War I was manufactured by the PE for the purpose of creating the first attempt at a world government (the League of

Nations). PE agent Col. Edward House in the CFR's *Foreign Affairs* (June 1923) wrote that "if war had not come in fierce and exaggerated form," the League would not have materialized. In John Kenneth Turner's *Shall It Be Again?* (1922), one finds that the J. P. Morgan firm had drawn up plans to scare Americans into joining the war (J. P. Morgan Bank had also backed Japan when it declared war on Russia in 1904). Turner also revealed that in 1914, France was ready for peace (meaning there would not be a world war), but that Morgan partner Robert Bacon dissuaded French leaders from discussing peace, because he said he and some American politicians could get the U.S. into the war on the side of France. The PE had to have World War I, and Rhodes' close ally, Lord Esher, told one of President Wilson's principal supporters, Henry Morgenthau, that American blood needed to be shed as soon as possible to get the U.S. into the war in 1917.

When the League failed to produce the desired world government, then a Second World War had to be manufactured to produce the United Nations, which was discussed long before the end of WWII. American (e.g., J. P. Morgan) and British banks funded German industries such as I.G. Farben from Hitler's early days. According to G. Edward Griffin, Farben "was the primary source of funding for Hitler [and] staffed and directed Hitler's intelligence section and ran the Nazi slave labor camps. ... During the Allied bombing raids over Germany, the factories and administrative buildings of I.G. Farben were spared upon instructions from the U.S. War Department." The War Department widely was staffed by agents of the PE, who had worked for Rockefeller's National City Bank, Rockefeller's Dillon, Read & Company, J. P. Morgan's Equitable Trust, etc.

Another PE agent, H. G. Wells, wrote in *The Shape Of Things To Come* (1933) that WWII would begin around 1939, which it did. How would he know this unless it was planned?

About this same time, the German General Staff developed

a secret plan that was described in CFR member Sumner Welles' *The Time For Decision* (1944). Welles revealed that the German General Staff "made detailed plans for a later renewal of its attempt to dominate the world ... when the favorable moment arrives ... [perhaps] two generations from now"—in other words, today! Welles went on to say "half the mechanism is secret and will so remain," and involves the theory of

> indirect complicity ... in three principal ways: (a) it will try to create doubts among the people of each country as to the ability, integrity, wisdom, or loyalty of their leading statesmen; (b) in critical moments it will attempt to paralyze or to diminish the capacity for cool thinking by the people as a whole; and (c) it will search each country for men who, through ambition, vanity, or personal interest, will be disposed to serve the causes. ... Agents of the German General Staff have already been naturalized, usually in two successive countries, so that their future activities will be less suspect. The majority of them are being trained to appear as men of large commercial or financial interests... over a period of years [gaining] a controlling influence in labor unions, in the banking world, in Chambers of Commerce, and, through these channels, an indirect influence in the press. ... When the right time comes, stimulate internal dissension sufficiently to destroy the morale of the people in those countries marked as victims.

If you think about it, the only reason for such a plan is that the Nazis would lose the war. If they won, they wouldn't have to wait for two generations for anything! This is where Colonel Stauffenberg's plot and its surprising openness make sense. Hitler's rise to power, World War II "in fierce and exaggerated form," and Hitler's demise, all were part of the PE's plan to create an environment favorable for establishing a world government (the U.N.).

No-win wars like in Korea and Vietnam were planned as well. In *U.S.A.* magazine (May 1951), Gen. Douglas MacArthur revealed: "I am convinced I was restrained in Korea by some secret Administration policy directive or strategy about which I was not informed." The PE through its agent, Gen. George Marshall, facilitated the Chinese communists coming to power in 1949. This was because as State Department Study Memorandum No. 7 (published under Rhodes scholar Secretary of State Dean Rusk in 1961) stated: "If the communist dynamic was greatly abated, the West might lose whatever incentive it has for world government."

The American loss in Vietnam (remember Freneau's 1792 revelation about planned war losses) was to undermine patriotism, thus making a world government more acceptable. On May 22, 1974, *The New York Times* published the 1973 findings of pollster and CFR member Daniel Yankelovich indicating only nineteen percent of college-educated youth and only thrty-five percent of non-college-educated youth between sixteen and twenty-five years of age thought patriotism is an important value.

Of course, the long drawn-out tragedy of Vietnam set the stage for the third try at world order, which was the title (*The Third Try at World Order*) of Rhodes scholar Harlan Cleveland's book in 1977, shortly after the end of the Vietnam War. In his book, CFR member Cleveland called for "changing Americans' attitudes and institutions"; for "complete disarmament (except for international soldiers)"; for "fairer distribution of worldly goods through a new International Economic Order"; and for "international standards for individual entitlement to food, health and education."

As the world entered the 1980s, it was the precise time H. G. Wells in *The Shape of Things To Come* in 1933 said the coming "World-State" would appear. The problem, though, was Wells said it would arise out of a great world conference in Basra, Iraq.

Thus, it was critical to have a war involving Iraq, and such a war was foreshadowed by President George H. W. Bush in his

February 28, 1990, speech in San Francisco where he exclaimed: "Time and again in this century, the political map of the world was transformed. And in each instance, a new world order came about through the advent of a new tyrant or the outbreak of a bloody global war, or its end." The tyrant Saddam Hussein of Iraq shortly thereafter was misled by U.S. ambassador to Iraq April Glaspie into thinking the U.S. would consider Iraq's action against Kuwait a matter between those two countries, not necessarily resulting in an American military response.

Of course, there was an American military response to Iraq's invasion of Kuwait, and President Bush delivered his famous "Toward a New World Order" address to Congress on September 11, 1990. According to Bob Woodward in *Shadow* (1999), in early January 1991 President Bush told his closest advisors, "We have to have a war." The Gulf War began January 17, 1991, but its objective was simply to remove Saddam's forces from Kuwait, not to remove him from power, which could open a special focus on Basra. That would be left to his son President George W. Bush with the American invasion of Iraq itself beginning March 20, 2003. When Iraq was then occupied, American forces policed most of the country. However, Basra was controlled by British forces, which made sense from the PE's perspective since it was Cecil Rhodes' plan to have a world government, and both he and H. G. Wells were British.

When Iraq becomes more stabilized, it will be a showcase for the PE's ability to control world events. Therefore, Basra logically will be the location of a future global conference that will plan the "World-State" foretold by H. G. Wells and desired by Cecil Rhodes and his PE allies.

What will the future World-State be like? In 1922, Wells wrote *A Short History of the World*, which was also the title of a book in A.D. 2000 by Australian professor Geoffrey Blainey, who has been honored by *Encyclopaedia Britannica*. Both Wells and Blainey have indicated there will be a world government, and in an article in the

*Sydney Morning-Herald* (September 8, 1988), Blainey was quoted as saying: "I am inclined to think that someday a world government will emerge and that it will not be palatable to those who value freedom but more palatable to those who value freedom from international war."

It is not coincidental that under secretary of state and Rhodes scholar Dean Rusk, State Department document number 7277 was published and titled "Freedom From War: The U.S. Program for General and Complete Disarmament in a Peaceful World." Yes, it will be very peaceful under the coming world socialist government, just as it is very peaceful today under the Chinese communist dictatorship. It will be "peaceful" because, like in China today, those who protest the loss of freedom will be "removed." As H. G. Wells wrote in *The New World Order* (1939): "We are living in the end of the sovereign states. ... In the great struggle to evoke a westernized world socialism, contemporary governments may vanish. ... Countless people ... will hate the new world order ... and will die protesting against it."

## The Power Elite's Use of War and Debt

Several hundred years ago, the Bank of England was established by money from the Bank of Amsterdam and the Dutch power elite, who also brought William and Mary to power in England in 1689. Within nine years, King William got the British Treasury in great debt to the Bank of England, following the PE's principle of "get them in debt" to control them. This principle was used throughout the eighteenth and nineteenth centuries via costly wars to control entire nations which had imperialist ambitions.

Tremendous fortunes were built during this time by the PE, primarily reflected in emerging oil cartels such as Standard Oil (Rockefellers) with Anglo-Iranian (worked with Rhodes/Milner Group) and Shell (Royal Dutch, William and Mary came to

England from Holland). By the early twentieth century, John D. Rockefeller had his agents in every hamlet of the U.S., and foundations (e.g., Rockefeller) were used to further the power elite's designs. Congressional Research director Norman Dodd said that minutes from a Carnegie Endowment meeting revealed the attitude that war would be a primary vehicle for accomplishing their goals.

Both presidents Woodrow Wilson and FDR have spoken and written about these powerful people who literally own our government. This PE has had its operatives in key positions, and a young Druid, Winston Churchill, conducted a study of what the U.S. reaction would be if a passenger liner with Americans on board were to be sunk by a German submarine. Some years later, British secretary of state Sir Edward Grey (close to the Rhodes/Milner Group) deliberately misled German Ambassador Lichnowsky to begin World War I. And Lord Esher (member of Cecil Rhodes' Circle of Initiates) plotted "to shed American blood as soon as possible" to get the U.S. into the war.

Why a war with Germany? This was done to weaken Germany militarily and economically as a threat to the PE's plans, including access to Middle East oil. After the war, Sir Percy Cox (Rhodes/Milner Group) carved up the Middle East into various nations, establishing Kuwait as a block to Iraq's access to the sea, thus controlling oil routes. The First World War was also fought to get nations in debt and to bring about the PE's League of Nations as a world government.

When the League wasn't successful, a second world war was needed, so the PE built up Germany again as well as imperialist Japan, even selling the latter scrap metal with which to build warships. Nazi officers were on many Standard Oil tankers to be sure they weren't sunk. And the German General Staff developed a secret plan to bring about the PE's control beginning in the 1990s (see Chapter 9 of Sumner Welles' *The Time for Decision*, 1944).

Prime Minister Churchill (who had a "secret circle") and FDR knew about the Japanese attack on Pearl Harbor in advance (see Skull & Bones member Henry Stimson's diary about FDR maneuvering Japan into firing the first shot). The Second World War also allowed the permanent stationing of U.S. forces in Germany and Japan.

After World War II, the PE finally fulfilled the promise of the Balfour Declaration to the Jews, and the nation of Israel was established in 1948. This was not due to any particular affinity for the Jewish people, but rather to have a militarily strong but economically dependent (and therefore subject to coercion) country in the midst of Arab oil nations. An example of Israel being able to check Arab military efforts can be seen with the Israeli victory in their 1967 war. But the PE's "management" of Israel can also be seen in Israel's failure a few years ago to crush Hezbollah, probably due to economic coercion (e.g., threats of no further loans or foreign investments).

The year after the founding of Israel, the PE in 1949 facilitated the success of the Chinese communists over Chinese nationalists, who relocated largely to Taiwan, thus allowing the permanent presence of U.S. forces there. The permanent stationing of U.S. troops in South Korea near the north of China and the south of the U.S.S.R. was facilitated by the deliberately "no-win" Korean War in the early 1950s.

I have quoted many times Lincoln Bloomfield's 1962 study for the State Department, in which he indicated that if the communist dynamic were greatly abated, the West might lose whatever incentive it has for world government. Thus, it was important to the PE that the U.S.S.R. and China be perceived as real threats so as to further the dialectical process that would synthesize Eastern communism and Western capitalism into a final world socialist government. Ford Foundation president H. Rowan Gaither in 1953 even told Norman Dodd (mentioned earlier) that they and others were under directives from the White House to so alter life in the U.S. as to make possible a comfortable merger with the Soviet Union.

Also in 1953, the independent elected Iranian leader, Mossadegh, was removed from office by the power elite (via the CIA and Allen Dulles) because he nationalized Iranian oil, which greatly displeased the oil cartel mentioned earlier. The year after Mohammad Mossadegh was ousted, the Dutch (remember Royal Dutch Shell mentioned earlier) hosted the first Bilderberg meeting where, according to William Jasper in *Global Tyranny ... Step By Step*, "the international ruling elite meet to scheme and palaver."

War was used by the PE again in the 1960s and 1970s with the Vietnam War serving more than one function. First, it served to distract from radical domestic changes the PE wanted, as described in James Kunen's *The Strawberry Statement*. In this book, he revealed ESSO (Rockefeller) money was used to try to "buy up a few radicals" to seem so extremely liberal, the populace would not notice the power elite's own move to the left (e.g., "ping pong diplomacy" opening up China to the West). Also, Vietnam was another deliberately "no-win" war that "turned off" youth from patriotic nationalism as part of the PE's created "generation gap." That this can be recognized as part of the PE's plan is evident from Philip Freneau's July 1792 *American Museum* article, where he warns the young American republic that getting people in debt and using military defeat (e.g., Vietnam War) were part of the elite's strategy to gain control of the U.S.

It was also toward the end of the Vietnam War that the PE's agent, Henry Kissinger, revealed how they think about us common folk when he stated that soldiers are simply "dumb animals" to be used in the furtherance of an administration's foreign policy decisions. That the Vietnam War wasn't a "real war" seems clear from the fact that the U.S. continued financially to assist the U.S.S.R. and China throughout the war, even though they were the two nations primarily responsible for North Vietnam's and the Viet Cong's ability to wage war against the U.S.

In the 1980s, the PE turned its attention to the Persian Gulf causing a prolonged war between Iraq and Iran (both sides were assisted by the U.S.). Iraq won this war but accrued great debt as a result, and when the PE denied Saddam Hussein loans to pay off the debt, he invaded Kuwait which he thought had given (not loaned) him the funds to conduct the war against Iran. In a repeat of Lord Grey's misleading Germany to begin World War I, American ambassador to Iraq April Glaspie seems to have misled Saddam into thinking he would not be opposed if he invaded Kuwait. This was all done to "set up" Saddam, whom the PE did not want to obtain undue influence over oil production in the Gulf region.

It was one thing to reduce Saddam's military strength in the first Gulf War, but it was quite another thing to persuade people to support an occupation of that nation. That would take a pretext or incident like 9/11, which Bush administration officials immediately tried to blame on Saddam. Remember that longtime Middle East CIA agent Robert Baer in *See No Evil* indicated that a high-ranking CIA officer said 9/11 would eventually be considered a "triumph" of the intelligence community, not a failure.

The prolonged chaos in Iraq has allowed U.S. troops to obtain a permanent military presence there in the region, which is what the PE wanted all along. The removal of the Taliban from power in Afghanistan after the attacks of 9/11 also facilitated the permanent presence of U.S. military forces in the Caspian region, likewise part of the PE's plan. According to famous author H. G. Wells in *The Shape of Things To Come* (1933), there will be eventually a conference in Basra, Iraq, which will bring to fruition the power elite's ultimate goal of a world socialist government.

This goal has been pursued for many years using primarily wars and debt. For recent examples concerning debt accrued by means other than war, see John Perkins' *An Economic Hit Man* and

Steve Hiatt's *A Game As Old As Empire.* Examples include the Philippines being told to borrow great sums of money to improve its infrastructure so that factories will locate there, but then cheaper labor is found in other countries, so Filipinos are left holding the bag. Also, the International Monetary Fund (IMF) and World Bank funnel loans to nations where dictators pocket the money in their offshore accounts, and the people of that country are left to pay the debt and restructure their economies along the lines required by the IMF and World Bank.

## The Power Elite's Use of Wars and Crises

When congressional Reece Committee research director Norman Dodd's legal assistant Kathryn Casey looked at the planning documents for the founding of the Carnegie Endowment, she found something quite revealing. She found that they determined war would be helpful in furthering their objectives. Relevant to this, Rene Wormser in *Foundations: Their Power and Influence* (1958)

wrote that the head of the endowment, Nicholas Murray Butler, used the endowment's funds to get the U.S. into World War I.

The year after the endowment was founded in 1910, Robert Minor's cartoon in the *St. Louis Post-Dispatch* in 1911 depicted members of the power elite (John D. Rockefeller, Andrew Carnegie, J. P. Morgan, etc.) welcoming Karl Marx and his "socialism" to Wall Street. The next year Woodrow Wilson ran for president, and his "handler" for the PE, Col. Edward M. House, assured his bosses that Wilson would support the Federal Reserve's establishment in 1913.

The year after that (1914), the PE arranged the first World War long before the assassination of Archduke Franz Ferdinand on June 28 by members of the Narodna Odbrana (Black Hand) secret society. On May 29, 1914, Colonel House in Berlin wrote to President Wilson: "Whenever England consents, France and Russia will close in on Germany and Austria." The trick would be to make Germany think England would not enter the war. This was done by British secretary of state Sir Edward Grey misleading German ambassador to England Prince Karl Max Lichnowsky. Grey was close to the (Lord Alfred) Milner Group which was executing power elite member Cecil Rhodes' plan for world government.

Milner was the power behind the scenes in British government. He, not Prime Minister David Lloyd George, actually ran British foreign affairs. Milner was favorably disposed to Marxian socialism, and pro-Bolshevist Sir Basil Zaharoff (an armaments dealer who had sold arms to both sides in several wars) was consulted by President Wilson and Prime Minister George before any major military operation. This is according to author Donald McCormick, who said Zaharoff sought to divert munitions away from anti-Bolshevists.

When World War I began, Helmuth Johannes Ludwig von Moltke was head of the German General Staff. Interestingly, he was married to Dorothy Rose-Innes, the daughter of Sir James Rose-Innes, a member of Rhodes' Association of Helpers, as was their son Helmuth James von Moltke.

It was important for the PE to drag the U.S. into the war, and so Lord Esher (executive committee member of Rhodes' secret Society of the Elect) wrote in his diary on August 3, 1917: "Can there be any doubt that the war has made for progress?" He followed this on August 11 with "Mr. Henry Morgenthau asked me to call on him. ... He was one of the principal supporters of President Wilson. ... They are ready to sacrifice the lives of American citizens. ... Mr. Morgenthau realizes the importance ... [of] shedding American blood at the earliest possible moment." Morgenthau would be a founding member of the Council on Foreign Relations (CFR), which was largely funded and staffed by J. P. Morgan and John D. Rockefeller interests.

One of the key connections to these interests was William Boyce Thompson, who in 1914 became the first full-term director of the Federal Reserve Bank of New York. And *The Washington Post* (February 2, 1918) reported: "William B. Thompson, who was in Petrograd from July until November 1917, has made a personal contribution of $1,000,000 to the Bolsheviki for the purpose of spreading their doctrine in Germany and Austria."

While in Russia from July to November 1917, Thompson was head of the Red Cross mission there. The Red Cross was heavily dependent upon Wall Street and especially J. P. Morgan interests for donations. Therefore, these interests were able to use the Red Cross to further their goals. Thompson's assistant, Cornelius Kelleher, is quoted in George Kennan's *Russia Leaves the War* as stating: "The Red Cross complexion of the mission was nothing but a mask." FDR advisor and Soviet agent in the 1940s Harry Hopkins was assistant to the general manager of the Red Cross in Washington, D.C. In December 1917, Raymond Robins succeeded Thompson as head of the Red Cross mission in Russia, and on December 26, Robins called Morgan senior partner Henry Davison (chairman of the War Council of the American Red Cross, whose son in 1920 would become a member of Skull & Bones) asking him to urge President Wilson to continue intercourse with the Bolshevik government.

Both Robins and his wife were associated with Bolshevik activities in the U.S. Robins was a protege of Colonel House and one of his heroes was Cecil Rhodes. According to Bruce Lockhart (sent to Russia by Lord Milner and Prime Minister George) in *British Agent* (1933), "Robins was the only man whom Lenin was always willing to see and who ever succeeded in imposing his own personality on the unemotional Bolshevik leader." Lenin capitulated to Robins' ultimatum to remove Saalkind as Assistant Commissar for Foreign Affairs.

Carroll Quigley in *Tragedy and Hope* (1966) wrote: "More than fifty years ago [before 1916] the Morgan firm decided to infiltrate the Left-wing political movements in the United States." And the Morgan-controlled American International Corporation (AIC) was probably the primary supporter of the Bolsheviks. On October 17, 1917, AIC director William Saunders (deputy chairman of the Federal Reserve Bank of New York) wrote to President Wilson: "I am in sympathy with the Soviet form of government as that best suited for the Russian people." Other AIC directors in 1917 were Pierre du Pont, J. Peter Grace, Otto Kahn, Percy Rockefeller (Skull & Bones member), Frank Vanderlip (president of Rockefeller's National City Bank), and others. Julius Hammer (chairman of Occidental Petroleum Corporation) and his son Armand (who was a Soviet citizen) were also strong supporters of the Soviets.

Colonel House in 1912 authored *Philip Dru: Administrator* promoting "socialism as dreamed of by Karl Marx." And one of his aides, Kenneth Durant, became assistant secretary for the Soviet Bureau in the U.S. When the premiers of France and Italy (Clemenceau and Orlando) later expressed concern about the Bolsheviks and their westward expansion, Colonel House in his diary wrote that he deliberately misled them into thinking there was nothing that could be done about it.

President Wilson was simply a puppet of the PE, manipulated by their agent Colonel House. And on November 28, 1917, Wilson ordered there should be no interference with the Bolsheviks' revolution. Not long thereafter, the U.S. legation in Bern, Switzerland, cabled Washington "asking why the president expresses support of

Bolsheviki, in view of rapine, murder and anarchy of these bands" (U.S. State Department decimal file 861.00/1305, March 15, 1918). What is telling about American members of the PE supporting the Bolsheviks is the fact that even before the war ended, Soviet troops were fighting and killing American soldiers in the Archangel region!

Robert Minor, whose cartoon I mentioned earlier, was a socialist who went to Russia in March 1918 and then worked in the Commissariat for Foreign Affairs. He even prepared propaganda against American soldiers and was arrested, but Colonel House and President Wilson intervened on his behalf and he was released without going to trial (probably because he was not doing anything different than Thompson and Robins).

Colonel House was managing the PE's plan to bring about "socialism as dreamed of by Karl Marx," and the First World War was a necessary part of that plan. After the war, the CFR was founded largely by Colonel House's group "the Inquiry," and in the CFR's *Foreign Affairs* (June 1923) Colonel House wrote: "If war had not come in 1914 in fierce and exaggerated form, the idea of an association of nations would probably have remained dormant, for great reforms seldom materialize except during great upheavals."

The first association of nations the PE planned, the League of Nations, didn't materialize as the world government they desired, and therefore a Second World War had to be arranged. In case you don't believe World War II was planned, how else do you explain that PE agent H. G. Wells in 1933 in his *The Shape of Things To Come* said in about six years the war would begin over a German-Polish dispute, and Germany invaded Poland on September 1, 1939, with Britain and France declaring war on Germany two days later? Moreover, how else do you explain PE agent Sir Julian Huxley on December 5, 1941, saying he hoped America and Japan would be at war "next week," and the attack on Pearl Harbor occurred Sunday, December 7, 1941, the first day of the next week? The PE knew that the second "association of nations," the U.N., formed after World War II, would also not be their desired world government, as H. G. Wells in *The Shape of Things To Come* said they would succeed on their third attempt resulting from a conference in Basra, Iraq. This is why the current war in Iraq was planned by the PE.

Cecil Rhodes' and the PE's goal was and still is the establishment of a world socialist government via linking regional economic arrangements, and Lenin and Stalin were important parts of this. In Vienna in January 1913, Stalin had advocated national loyalties become subservient to regions. And the year after Colonel House's *Foreign Affairs* article appeared, Stalin in April 1924 said that according to Leninism "a single world system of economy constitutes the material basis for the victory of socialism."

It was also in this time (1920s) that Jean Monnet developed his plans for the first of these economic regions, the European Union. His lawyer was a young John J. McCloy, the successor to Colonel House in managing the PE's plan. In 1936, McCloy sat in Hitler's box at the Berlin Olympics, and during the 1940s Secretary of War Henry Stimson (Skull & Bones member who initiated George H. W. Bush into Skull & Bones) questioned "whether anyone in the Administration ever acted without having a word with McCloy."

From 1953 to 1970, McCloy was the chairman of the CFR, during which time he swam with Soviet dictator Nikita Khrushchev in late July 1961 at the Black Sea. In the early 1950s, Frederick Schuman in *The Commonwealth of Men: An Inquiry Into Power, Politics, and World Government* wrote that one way permanent peace is attainable is "through the voluntary merging of sovereignties in a global polity, with a World-State emerging out of agreement."

McCloy was followed as CFR chairman by David Rockefeller from 1970 to 1985. During that time, Bahai leader John Ferraby in

*All Things Made New* (1975) wrote similarly to Schuman that "we have entered a new era, in which the unification of mankind can be adequately organized only by a world state."

"World State" and "New World Order" were both terms used by H. G. Wells to refer to a world government. This concept was adopted by a number of people, and in *Journeys for a Better World* (1994), U.N. Secretariat official Jean Richardot declared that "a prosperous united world representing a true New World Order could only be attained step by step. While we are still far from world government, we must first focus on essential issues that work in that direction."

As I have written before, a single global currency is an important part of this effort to achieve a world government. In that regard Sarah Perry (director of Visa's Strategic Investment Program) is quoted in *The Single Global Currency* (2006) as remarking in 2001: "When Visa was founded twenty-five years ago, the founders saw the world as needing a Single Global Currency for exchange. Everything we've done from a global perspective has been about trying to put one piece in place after another to fulfill that global vision."

And how will the single global currency be brought about? Nobel prize winner Robert Mundell (known as "the Father of the Euro") in a speech titled "A Decade Later: Asia New Responsibilities in the International Monetary System" delivered in Seoul, South Korea, May 2–3, 2007, revealed: "International monetary reform usually becomes possible only in response to a felt need and the threat of a global crisis. The global crisis would have to involve the dollar," and a single global currency would be "a contingency" to this global dollar crisis. As you are aware, the dollar is currently in crisis, plummeting in value.

David Rockefeller in his *Memoirs* (2002) admitted being part of a secret cabal conspiring with others to bring about a world government. This plan was revealed 100 years ago by Robert Hugh

Benson in *Lord of the World* (1907), in which he wrote that "in 1917 ... communism really began. ... The new order began then." Ten years before the 1917 Bolshevik Revolution in Russia, Benson foretold it. Benson also wrote of a future European Parliament, American socialism, and "the final scheme of Western Free Trade" occurring after 1989. He revealed that in the end, continent would unite with continent, the appearance of peace would deceive many, and that "the Humanity Religion was the only one."

This final replacement of God by man as the final moral authority will characterize biblical end times. As I mentioned in my December 31, 2007, NewsWithViews.com column "Iraq, Iran, and Pakistan," Ezekiel 38:5 indicates that in the prophecy regarding Gog and Magog, Persians (Iranians) will come against Israel. According to Joseph Farah, recently on Israeli secular television were in-depth reports on Gog and Magog describing the forces that will be aligned against each other in Revelation 20. On one side will be Israel, the U.S., Britain, France, and Germany. On the other side will be Iran, Russia, China, Syria, and North Korea. The Gog and Magog war is also mentioned in the Koran in Sura 18:94 and 21:96, and the Iranian mullahs have also recently been referring to this. According to the Koran, the people paid tribute to "The Conqueror" Dhu al Qarnayn, popularly understood to be Alexander the Great (who was at the time considered Lord of the West, the East, Persia, etc.), to erect barriers against the wild and lawless tribes of Central Asia (Mongols from Kazakhstan, Uzbekistan, etc.). However, in a prognostication of the approaching "judgment" of the world, the tribes break through the barriers when the people degenerate morally, and the wild tribes "swiftly swarm from every hill" against the formerly protected people written about in the Koran.

Writing of Alexander the Great in this part of the world was Rhodes Trust member Rudyard Kipling in *The Man Who Would Be King*. What is happening is the unfolding of Rhodes' plan for world government, which in turn will lead to the fulfillment of end times biblical prophecy.

## Transformation by Crises and Syntheses

Some years ago, Ervin Laszlo of the U.N. Institute for Training and Research spoke about how various crises and a change in man could create a critical instability resulting in a transformation to a New World Order. As I've written before, the power elite wants a New World Order with ultimate control over us. However, they have to have an excuse for intervening in our lives. This is accomplished by the use of crises (followed by syntheses), and here we focus on domestic and international examples of this process.

In Naomi Klein's *The Shock Doctrine* (2007), she explains the use of crises to promote a "new colonialism" around the world. She indicates the doctrine works as follows:

> The original disaster [crisis]—the coup, the terrorist attack, the market meltdown, the war, the tsunami, the hurricane puts the entire population into a state of collective shock. The falling bombs, the bursts of terror, the pounding winds, serve to soften up whole societies much as the blaring music and blows in the torture cells soften up prisoners. Like the terrorized prisoner who gives up the names of comrades and renounces his faith, shocked societies often give up things they would otherwise fiercely protect.

Domestically, the PE uses "crises," such as in the area of mental health, as a pretext for intervention. According to the U.S. Surgeon-General's 1999 Report on Mental Health, over twenty percent of all children aged nine to seventeen meet the criteria for a mental health diagnosis. This led to President George W. Bush forming the New Freedom Commission on Mental Health

(NFCMH) in 2002, and two years later it produced "Achieving the Promise: Transforming Mental Health Care in America" (remember the word "transforming" used here). The document called for establishing statewide systems to screen all Americans beginning at birth. One state after another began to comply, with the Indiana legislature, for example, on July 1, 2006, amending the school code to consolidate all mental health services "from birth to twenty-two years of age."

Educational programs have been a primary vehicle for screening, as the National Institute of Mental Health (NIMH) Research Center at the University of Michigan produced "Social Risks and Psychological Health: Strengthening Mental Health Screening in Head Start Programs: The Family Development Project" saying that "our screening tools have been incorporated as part of Head Start's regular enrollment procedures." But Head Start was just the beginning, as Nathaniel Lehrman, M.D., in "The Dangers of Mental Health Screening" (*Journal of American Physicians and Surgeons,* Fall 2006) reported that according to the NFCMH, "All American parents will receive notice from their youngsters' schools of the new screening program during the 2005–2006 school year. It will test for mental illness in the 52 million students and 6 million adults working in schools, and expect to find at least 6 million in need of treatment."

And not to miss any avenues of intervention, Medicaid has also been used in this process, as Carey Goldberg of the *Boston Globe* (December 27, 2007) reported in "Mental Screening for Young to Begin" that "annual checkups for the nearly half a million Massachusetts children on Medicaid will carry a new requirement: Doctors must offer simple questionnaires to detect warning signs of possible mental health problems, from autism in toddlers to depression in teens."

Concerning autism, Organic Consumers Organization on February 25, 2008, reported that "after years of insisting that there is no evidence linking vaccines and autism, the U.S. government has quietly conceded a vaccine-autism case in the Court of Federal Claims." The court heard a child's claim against the government that mercury-containing vaccines were the cause of her autism. And the court "concluded that compensation is appropriate." Despite this finding, states like Maryland require all students to be vaccinated for chicken pox and hepatitis B, and *The Washington Post* (November 14, 2007) reported that "the parents of more than 2,300 students in Prince George's County, MD, could face fines of $50 a day and ten days in jail if their children do not meet the state's immunization requirements."

Note in the first part of this article the emphasis on "mental illness" and the word "transforming." The PE emphasizes these and wants screening at ever earlier ages because it wants to transform people's values which are shaped at a very early age. Not too long ago in education, William Spady's "Transformational" OBE (outcome-based education) stresses changing students' values. And Spady's values are revealed in his September 1987 document, "Future Trends: Considerations in Developing Exit Outcomes," in which he states: "Despite the historical trend toward intellectual enlightenment and cultural pluralism, there has been a major rise in religious and political orthodoxy, intolerance, fundamentalism, and conservatism with which young people will have to be prepared to deal."

In addition to education, the PE has also used, domestically and internationally, religion to accomplish their goal of changing people's values. Historically, in the July 1908 edition of *The Hibbert Journal,* the "Father of Progressive Education" John Dewey wrote: "Religion and our schools" in which he revealed:

> Our schools ... are performing an infinitely significant religious work. They are performing the social unity out of which in the end genuine religious unity must grow. ... Religion... associated

with … dogmatic beliefs … we see disappearing. … It is the part of men to labor persistently and patiently for the clarification and development of the positive creed of life implicit in democracy and in science, and to work for the transformation of all practical instrumentalities of education till they are in harmony with these ideas.

In 1934, Dewey further explained his intended "religious unity" by authoring *A Common Faith,* in which he explained: "I cannot understand how any realization of the democratic ideal as a vital moral and spiritual ideal in human affairs is possible without surrender of the conception of the basic division to which supernatural Christianity (separating sheep and goats) is committed." This was the year after Dewey co-authored the first *Humanist Manifesto.*

Regarding religion today, Brian McLaren is the leader of the Emergent Church. He's a product of Bob Buford's Leadership Network, and Buford was mentored by management guru Peter Drucker. In Discernment Ministry's *Herescope* blog (January 24, 2006), Drucker's model for societal "transformation" is identified as communitarianism, which emphasizes the common good.

Relevant to the common (public) good, transformation and feudalism (to which the PE wants to return), Drucker in "The Age of Social Transformation" (*The Atlantic Monthly,* November 1994), wrote: "What do institutions have to do to advance the public good? This, though nobody seems to realize it, is a demand to return to the old pluralism, the pluralism of feudalism." Drucker is a product of the Frankfurt School (receiving his Ph.D. from the University of Frankfurt before coming to the U.S. in 1937), which has played a critical role in reshaping attitudes, values, and beliefs here. Concerning this, in his article Drucker refers to "knowledge workers" as the "newly emerging dominant group" and he said displaced industrial workers "at the very least have to change their basic attitudes, values and beliefs." He further explained "that knowledge has become the key resource means that there is a world economy, and that the world economy, rather than the national economy, is in control" (another goal of the PE).

Relevant to Brian McLaren and the Emergent Church movement, Drucker also wrote:

> The organizations that have shown the capacity to grow are radically new. They are the "pastoral" churches, which ... put the spiritual energies of their members (especially educated knowledge workers) to work on the social challenges and social problems of the community. ... The "product" of a church is a churchgoer whose life is being changed. The task of social-sector organizations (including pastoral churches) is to create human health and well being.

In Brian McLaren's 2007 book *Everything Must Change: Jesus, Global Crises and a Revolution of Hope* (note the words "change" and "crises"), he also emphasizes the "common good" and refers to "radical rethinking." Robert Schuller on January 17–19, 2008, hosted a "Rethink Conference" attended by President George H. W. Bush and Kay Warren, wife of church-growth leader Rick Warren. According to the conference executive director Bill Dallas, they "confronted outdated and preconceived ideas."

In McLaren's book, he states that for millions of young adults, "the Christian religion appears to be a failed religion" because it has "specialized in dealing with 'spiritual' needs," failing to address systemic injustice, poverty, ecological crisis, and other societal and global dysfunctions. This sounds like the leftist Catholics' old "Liberation Theology" claim. It also sounds similar to what co-founder of Global Education Associates Patricia Mische said at a November 9–11, 1984, symposium "Toward A Global Society," where she spoke on "The Spiral of Spiritual/Social Transformation." She pronounced: "Traditional religion is failing to speak to problems in our society. The need for a New World Order is our greatest challenge and opportunity. ... We see resistance to change—resistance to the New Age processes."

McLaren in his book continued to explain that this failed Christian religion's threats of Hell "lose their effect when those making the threats seem a little defensive, deranged, out of touch, manic. ..." Note that he's saying they are mentally ill! This is similar to New Ager Marilyn Ferguson in *The Aquarian Conspiracy: Personal and Social Transformation in the 1980s* (1980) saying that if people will get rid of "crippling belief systems," they can have a "transformation of consciousness" and find "sanity within." More recently, it sounds like Eckhart Tolle's *A New Earth: Awakening To Your Life's Purpose* (2005) promoted by Oprah's Book Club. He asserts that all of those expressing the certainty that "I am right and you are wrong" are a "dangerous thing in religions." It reflects a "collective mental illness." Tolle characterizes "sin" as simply "missing the point" of human existence and suggests that "Eastern wisdom teachings" allow us to "let go of dogmas" and "rigid belief systems." He also relates that in *The Holy Bible* "a new Heaven" actually refers to "the emergence of a transformed state of human consciousness." Note again the terms "mental illness" and "transformed."

Relevant to "wisdom teachings" and "transformation," New Age workers Corinne McLaughlin and Gordon Davidson (who has worked for Lucis Trust, formerly Lucifer Publishing) have taught "Transformational Politics" at American University and authored *Spiritual Politics* (1994). In their book, they wrote:

> The new transformational paradigm is based on certain key ideas which have long been part of the Ageless Wisdom tradition ... including creating a synthesis out of adversarial positions, synthesizing the best of hierarchy and democracy for real empowerment, and searching for common ground and the

good of the whole. ... Transformational politics requires a shift in contemporary consciousness.

In their book, there are sections titled "Synthesis as a Way of Life" and "A Synthesis of Liberalism and Conservatism." The authors also refer positively to the communitarian movement and explain that "The Ageless Wisdom teaches that the synthesis of hierarchy and democracy is the next evolutionary step for humanity."

Both Brian McLaren and Rick Warren (mentioned earlier) recently attended the World Economic Forum at Davos, Switzerland, where members of the PE also usually are in attendance. Warren is a CFR member who was also mentored by Peter Drucker, and who leads the Purpose Driven movement (note the word "purpose" is also in Tolle's book title). Like McLaren, Warren promotes a "new spirituality" that emphasizes a concern about global poverty, etc. I believe that to the extent this shift in emphasis occurs in churches, they will be "transformed" more and more into simply social service agencies. Relevant to this, in his November 14, 2007, "Ministry Toolbox," Warren tells his trained pastors: "You've got to protect the unity of your church. If that means getting rid of troublemakers, do it." By "troublemakers" he's referring to the fundamentalist or traditionalist "old pillars who only hold things up."

In Joseph Farah's WorldNetDaily column of November 30, 2007, he asks, "Why does Rick Warren eagerly seek to find common ground with Muslim leaders while, at the same time, so ruthlessly advocating the disfellowship of Christian believers?" Warren has even complimented Syria, although that nation's leaders have facilitated radical Muslim (Hezbollah and Hamas) attacks against Israel.

The PE considers Warren, McLaren, Tolle, and others like them, useful for their purposes, which includes ostracizing orthodox religious believers whether Christian or Jewish. In the Middle

East, for example, using the Delphi Technique, orthodox Jews are portrayed as recalcitrants, unwilling to compromise in order to obtain peace. Simultaneously, a dialectical process is used similar to communism being used as an antithesis to capitalism in order to achieve the synthesis (compromise) of a world socialist government.

As I've written before, CFR member Lincoln Bloomfield, in a study prepared for Secretary of State Dean Rusk (Rhodes scholar) in the Kennedy administration, wrote that if the communist dynamic (threat) were greatly abated, the West would lose whatever incentive it has for world government. Today in the Middle East, the same technique is being applied because if the radical Islamic threat of Hezbollah and Hamas were greatly abated, Israel would lose whatever incentive it has for world government.

The PE through its agent Javier Solana might have "persuaded" by economic means (loans and investments would not be forthcoming) Israeli prime minister Ehud Olmert not to launch a crippling blow against Hezbollah in their last major confrontation in Lebanon, thus maintaining the "unabated threat" against Israel. Afterward, Olmert, the Palestinian leaders, Secretary of State Condoleezza Rice and others are reportedly engaged in secret negotiations even to divide Jerusalem. This is all to weary Jews and Palestinians to compromise their principles and sign a peace agreement.

As Vice President Dick Cheney at the time stated, a Middle East peace agreement will require "painful compromises on both sides." However, it is part of the PE's plan to "transform" the Middle East through solving the conflict ("crisis") between Israelis and radical Muslims.

This will lead to the formation of a Middle Eastern economic region, which can then be linked with others (e.g., the European Union, African Union, ASEAN, forthcoming North American Union, etc.) to form a global economic union with a global currency, all managed by a world socialist government. This was explained in *The Single Global Currency* (2006) by Morrison Bonpasse (president of the Single Global Currency Association) when he wrote:

> The world is ready to begin preparing for a Single Global Currenty, just as Europe prepared for the Euro and as the Arabian Gulf countries are preparing for their common currency. After the goal of a Single Global Currency is established by countries representing a significant proportion of the world's GDP, then the project can be pursued like its regional predecessors.

And that this will have to be managed by a world government was explained by Robert Mundell (known as "Father of the Euro") in his 2003 lecture, "The International Monetary System and the Case for a World Currency," in which he revealed that "a global single currency could not be achieved without a global government to enforce it."

## Threats Used for Coercive Compliance

The movie *Brotherhood of the Rose* described how intelligence agencies, not national governments, actually worked together to control the world. In reality, the PE, not national governments, control the world using threats to coerce compliance with their will. Most people view world events in terms of the U.S. or NATO versus Russia or some other adversarial combination. However, the PE operates internationally above any nation and is comprised of individuals from the U.S., Europe, Russia, China, etc. who have no national loyalties, but rather are committed to their own power and control. At any given time, they may employ the military of any country to create a "threatening" situation in order to coerce compliance with their objectives. An economic threat may also be used, as Israel is militarily threatened by Iran, and the E.U. probably threatened Israeli prime minister Ehud Olmert with fewer investments and loans if Israel didn't stop its final retaliation against Hezbollah in Lebanon. Similarly, the U.S. doesn't have a free hand against communist China because the Chinese own a lot of our debt. The U.S. also can't simply withdraw from the global economy (which was created by the PE) because that would be disastrous economically (the stock market and people's 401Ks would crash because of heavy investments overseas). Sucking China into the global economy is likewise a goal of the PE, because once the Chinese economy is integrated with others, they can be threatened with instability as well if they fail to comply with the PE's wishes.

The threat against the West in general has most often been from communism, as Lincoln Bloomfield's report to Secretary of State Dean Rusk (Rhodes scholar) indicated that the West might lose whatever incentive it has for world government (which is the PE's ultimate goal) if the communist dynamic were greatly abated. But globally, threats can be non-communist as well, as India feels threatened by Pakistan and vice versa (watch Kashmir in the future).

Oil is a major component of the PE's threat mechanism. Oil-rich countries like Venezuela have felt militarily threatened by Colombian incursion, Kuwait and Saudi Arabia militarily were threatened by Iraq's Saddam Hussein, and Libya was bombed by the U.S.

Historically, Iran's democratically elected leader was overthrown by revolution in the early 1950s because he nationalized the nation's oil supply. The PE instigated the revolution which put into power the puppet Shah of Iran with the blessing of Ayatollah Kashani. When the Shah was no longer useful, a revolution instituted by the PE replaced him with Ayatollah Khomeini (mentored by Kashani). Today, regarding its oil and gas, Iran seeks military and economic allies in Russia and China because it feels threatened by the U.S. and Israel.

Concerning Afghanistan, PE agent Zbigniew Brzezinski lured the Soviets there in the late 1970s as part of a PE plan regarding Caspian oil and gas. American forces conducted maneuvers in Kazakhstan in 1995, two years before Brzezinski's *The Grand Chessboard* (1997) was published describing the new "Great Game" for energy supplies in that region. The Soviet puppet in Afghanistan was replaced by the Taliban, and Al Qaeda was originally supported by the U.S. The Taliban balked at complying with the PE's wishes regarding a pipeline from the Caspian region, thus resulting in a threat by the U.S. to which the Taliban's ally, Al Qaeda, responded on 9/11/2001. The attack by Al Qaeda also served as part of an unending terrorist threat that prompted the American people to give up some of their liberties (another PE goal) in the Patriot and Homeland Security Acts. The attack also presented the "truly massive and widely perceived direct external threat" that Brzezinski said in his book was necessary "to fashion a consensus on foreign policy issues," such as attacking Afghanistan to achieve the PE's oil and gas pipelines from the Caspian region. This was achieved by installing a compliant puppet, Karzai, as head of the new Afghan government.

In Yugoslavia, the situation was similar, as Slobodan Milosevic was standing in the way of a trade route linking the European Union with the planned Mediterranean Union (including Arab nations and Israel). He was also standing in the way of a new pipeline planned from Baku (Azerbaijan) on the Caspian Sea, then across the Black Sea through Kosovo down through Albania to the Adriatic Sea where it could be shipped to the West and around the world. Thus, the PE's "spontaneous" revolution for independence in Kosovo, to which Milosovic reacted when CIA-trained Kosovo Liberation Army (KLA) members (also supported by Al Qaeda) assassinated Serbian police, mayors, etc. This gave NATO (headed militarily by Rhodes scholar Gen. Wesley Clark and politically by Javier Solana, a product of Rhodes scholars Bill Clinton, Strobe

Talbott, and Richard Gardner) the "humanitarian crisis" it needed to attack Milosevic, killing a lot of innocent civilians as well.

Another pipeline from Baku (Azerbaijan) through Georgia and then Turkey to the Mediterranean Sea also resulted in another "spontaneous" revolution for independence by South Ossetia within Georgia. This time, the "spontaneous" revolutionaries were allied with Russia. This gave the U.S.-funded and trained Georgians the threat they needed to react militarily, killing about two thousand South Ossetian civilians and sending another forty thousand refugees into Russia. This, in turn, gave the Russians the threat they needed to crush the Georgians militarily. In June 2008, long before military action, PE agent Brzezinski warned of "cases of possible threats by Russia, directed at Georgia with the intention of taking control over the Baku-Ceyhan pipeline." PE agent Vladimir Putin could count on NATO's non-response because he could easily once again cut off Germany's, Poland's, etc. natural gas pipeline from Russia.

The PE doesn't want any nation or group of nations to be too strong or independent. This is why during and after WWII, the Soviets were given nuclear weapons material by FDR advisor Harry Hopkins, and communist Chinese were brought to power by Gen. George Marshall, both nations then serving as threats to the U.S. This is why an independent Iran in the early 1950s had to be undermined. It's why the U.S. had to not win in Korea and lose in Vietnam, and why the Soviets had to lose in Afghanistan. It's why the U.S. had to be threatened by terrorists, why Saddam Hussein had to be ousted when he didn't succumb to the will of "the international community," and why Slobodan Milosevic had to be removed from power for the same reason (the examples of Hussein and Milosevic serve to coerce other potentially independent leaders into compliance with the PE's will). And it's why NATO's expansion eastward toward Georgia was resisted by Russia, resulting in the current (and probably lasting) stalemate there.

In case you doubt the goal is a stalemate in Georgia, read carefully what PE agent Brzezinski wrote in his *The Grand Chessboard* relevant to Caspian oil, gas, and minerals. After referring several times to "ruling national elites," he explained "that America's primary interest is to help ensure that no single power comes to control this geopolitical space (Eurasia) and that the global community has unhindered financial and economic access to it." Now, one would think that Brzezinski as a former American national security advisor (and current Obama advisor) would like it if the U.S. (a "single power") controlled this geopolitical space, but that's not what he said. Rather, he emphasized "no single power" should control it. Remember that Brzezinski was David Rockefeller's first director of the Trilateral Commission, and Rockefeller in his *Memoirs* (2002) acknowledged about himself that he is "part of a secret cabal working against the best interests of the United States ... conspiring with others around the world to build a more integrated global political and economic structure—one world."

As long as no nation or group of nations becomes too strong or independent, the PE will maintain its power and control. Military and economic (cutoff of energy supplies) threats keep nations compliant with the will of the PE, which seeks to control the activities of nations and move them inexorably into regional economic unions to be linked ultimately into a world socialist government under the PE's control. In order that Americans accept this world socialist government, the PE increasingly has to move the U.S. toward socialism. This is being done via economic crises such as the recent federal takeover of Fannie Mae, Freddie Mac, and American International Group (AIG) some years ago. Government takeover of such major financial institutions is definitely a move toward classical economic socialism. Nouriel Roubini, professor of Economics and International Business at New York University, has suggested we may enter a global recession, and banks may have to be nationalized—another step toward socialism and fulfillment of the PE's plan. Also, the announcement on September 19, 2008, that the federal government is going to bailout Wall Street meant that the taxpayer would pick up the tab for all that debt. This will mean inflation (an indirect form of taxation) and a devaluing of the dollar (another part of the PE's plan to institute regional currencies like the Amero).

As I've written before, the PE has not only economic and political goals, but religious as well. They have a "theology of power," and facilitating this is "The Family," a somewhat secretive organization which began in the 1930s with definite fascist leanings. Over the decades, they have characterized even some brutal dictators as "men of God." The dictators respond favorably because The Family emphasizes to them (and everyone else) Romans 13:1 which states: "… For there is no power but of God: the powers that be are ordained of God." In the U.S., although invitations to the annual National Prayer Breakfast appear to come from the White House, it is actually organized (since 1953) by The Family and often has non-Christian speakers. Over the decades, powerful Republicans and Democrats have been associated with The Family. And Jeff Sharlet, author of *The Family* (2008), claims Hillary Clinton is considered a "friend" of this organization, which has formed a network of powerful leaders around the world. The PE's goal is global, economic, political, and religious power and control, which they use toward achieving a world socialist government and a one-world religion.

# Chapter 9

# Think You Have a Choice?

In Carroll Quigley's book *Tragedy and Hope* (1966) about Cecil Rhodes and the PE, he expresses his support for the PE and says there really should be no significant differences between the two major political parties. Similarly, Skull & Bones (SB) member William Whitney in the late nineteenth century developed a plan whereby the PE would finance both major political parties and have them alternate power so the public thinks it has a choice when it really doesn't.

The first SB member to be elected president was Republican William Howard Taft a century ago in 1908. His opponent, Democrat William Jennings Bryan was also acceptable to the globalist PE because he promised tariff reduction and favored beginning the income tax.

In 1912, SB member Taft ran again, but was defeated by Democrat Woodrow Wilson who was a PE puppet managed by its agent Col. Edward M. House, a promoter of "socialism as dreamed of by Karl Marx." This is because the PE was interested in establishing a Federal Reserve to get the country in debt.

Wilson was re-elected in 1916 with the theme, "He kept us out of war," although secret plans had already been made to enter World War I on the side of Britain and the Allies. This was discussed by Lord Esher (a member of Cecil Rhodes' secret Society of the Elect) and a chief Wilson financial backer and PE member, Henry Morgenthau. Wilson's opponent, Charles Evans Hughes, was guaranteed to lose because he failed to renounce support from German-American and Irish-American groups critical of Wilson's pro-British policies.

In 1920, Warren Harding was elected president. Although he was a patriotic nationalist opposed to the League of Nations, he was controlled by party bosses "owned" by the PE. His opponent, James Cox, was acceptable to the PE because of his support of the Covenant of the League of Nations.

Calvin Coolidge was elected president in 1924 with the support of the PE, who approved his advocacy of a world court, arms limitation, and international cooperation to maintain peace. His opponent, John Davis, was also acceptable to the PE because he advocated disarmament and the League of Nations.

In 1928, Herbert Hoover was elected president because he continued Coolidge's foreign policy. His opponent, Al Smith, was also acceptable to the PE because his protégé was PE puppet Franklin D. Roosevelt (FDR). Although Hoover was acceptable to the PE, he was defeated in 1932 by FDR who was greatly influenced by the Council on Foreign Relations (CFR). On November 21, 1933, FDR wrote PE agent Colonel House that they both knew the PE "owned" the U.S.

Colonel House's promotion of socialism fit with FDR's policies, which were described as socialist by Al Smith in 1936. In that year, FDR won re-election over Alf Landon who proposed no alternatives to FDR's socialist programs, thus ensuring his defeat during those hard times.

Similarly, in 1940 the PE (J. P. Morgan interests and Lord Lothian of Cecil Rhodes' secret society) had Wendell Willkie run against FDR so that Roosevelt's re-election would be assured. After the election, Willkie went on missions for FDR and wrote *One World* (1943) advocating world government.

FDR won re-election again in 1944 after doing the PE's bidding by making a secret deal with Stalin on December 1, 1943, to give the Soviets Poland, Latvia, Lithuania, Estonia, etc. after World War II. FDR's opponent, Thomas Dewey, was also acceptable to the PE because he, like FDR, advocated an international organization (U.N.) to maintain world peace.

In 1948, Harry Truman was elected president. Though most people remember Truman as an all-American fellow, he was actually a supporter of world government, carrying in his pocket Lord Tennyson's poem "Locksley Hall" about a "Federation of the World." This made him acceptable to the PE, as was his 1948 opponent, Thomas Dewey, mentioned already.

In 1952, Dwight Eisenhower was elected president and, like Truman, he is perceived as a strong nationalist. Actually, he was puppet of PE managers and CFR leaders John Foster Dulles and his brother Allen Dulles. "Ike" was chosen by the PE because he was a globalist, advocating a "global flag" according to the July 24, 1951, *Chicago Tribune*. His opponent, CFR member Adlai Stevenson, was also a globalist who wanted to continue FDR's New Deal programs, thus making him acceptable to the PE.

Eisenhower was re-elected in 1956, later supporting a federal Atlantic Union and an international school "purged of national bias." His opponent was again Adlai Stevenson.

In 1960, John Kennedy became president and was acceptable to the PE because he was a globalist, advocating complete disarmament, deferring to a new U.N. peace force. His opponent, Richard Nixon, was also a globalist and CFR member who supported a federal Atlantic Union as desired by the PE. In 1947, Congressman Nixon had introduced a resolution to allow the U.N. to enact, interpret, and enforce world law. In 1964, Lyndon Johnson won the presidency, expanding the PE's no-win Vietnam War that diminished patriotic values among American young adults. His opponent was Barry Goldwater, who was a rarity, not acceptable to the PE, which conducted a major media campaign scaring the public that Goldwater would start a nuclear war if elected.

In 1968, Nixon became president after writing in the CFR's *Foreign Affairs* of nations' disposition "to evolve regional approaches to development needs and to the evolution of a new world order," a key element of Cecil Rhodes' secret society's plan "to take the government of the whole world." Nixon further endeared himself to the PE by telling Rhodes scholar reporter Howard Smith that he (Nixon) was a Keynesian (socialist) in economics. Nixon's opponent, Hubert Humphrey, was acceptable to the PE because he had supported FDR and LBJ's policies regarding the Vietnam War.

Republican Nixon won re-election in 1972 against George McGovern, whom the PE set up to lose overwhelmingly because of his extreme anti-war views. This was necessary at this time because the PE wanted Nixon to open the door to communist China via PE agent and CFR member Henry Kissinger. In 1976, it was time for the PE's "alternation of power" mentioned at the beginning of this chapter. Democrat Jimmy Carter became president, winning over Republican Gerald Ford who had simply filled out Nixon's second term and wasn't very knowledgeable, though he was a CFR member and also acceptable to the PE. The PE had groomed Carter as a globalist, having Trilateral Commission (TC) director and CFR member Zbigniew Brzezenski become his national security advisor and many CFR members part of his administration.

Ronald Reagan defeated Carter in 1980 and is perceived as a nationalist. However, the PE "persuaded" him to have globalist and SB member George H. W. Bush (who sponsored a federal Atlantic Union in Congress in 1969) as his vice president. The PE also knew Reagan had been a member of the World Federalist Association, and during a May 28–30, 1983, G7 economic summit, Reagan pleased the PE by claiming, "Only a world currency will work." This assured his re-election the next year (1984) against Walter Mondale, who was also acceptable to the PE because he was a CFR and TC member.

In 1988, globalist George H. W. Bush became president and proclaimed the need for a "new world order." Once again, the PE provided a soft opponent in Michael Dukakis, whom the PE had surrounded with CFR advisors (seven of his eight foreign policy advisors).

In 1992, it was once again time for the PE's "alternation of power," so Republican Bush lost to Democrat Bill Clinton, who was mentored at Georgetown University by Prof. Carroll Quigley mentioned earlier. Clinton was a Rhodes scholar who supported world government. The PE wanted NAFTA, GATT, and the World Trade Organization, and Clinton, unlike Bush, could persuade enough Democrats to vote for them.

Bill Clinton won re-election in 1996 over Bob Dole who was endorsed by Rhodes scholar and CFR member James Woolsey, former Clinton CIA director. Dole was also acceptable to the PE as he was greatly beholden to globalists such as Dwayne Andreas, head of Archer-Daniels-Midland, which was founded by SB member Thomas Daniels.

Alternating power once again, SB member and globalist George W. Bush became president in 2000, defeating Vice President Al Gore. Gore's father was vice president of Occidental Petroleum under Armand Hammer, who was close to all Soviet dictators. Vice President Gore was also acceptable to the PE, and on October 12, 1998, announced his globalist "Declaration of Interdependence."

In 2004, the PE saw to it that Bush's re-election was assured as his opponent, fellow globalist and SB member John Kerry (CFR member), ran a lackluster campaign. Regarding the 2008 presidential election, I have in articles on NewsWithViews.com explained how senators John McCain and Barack Obama were both acceptable to the PE and were surrounded by CFR advisors.

In the 2012 election, while talk show hosts Rush Limbaugh, Sean Hannity, Glenn Beck, and others said Obama would lose due to high unemployment, I predicted he would win because he is important to the fulfillment of the secret Nazi plan, and he was opposed by Mitt Romney, who was acceptable to the PE because he could be relied upon not to promote the repeal of NAFTA and GATT.

In the upcoming 2016 election, Republican Jeb Bush would be the favorite of the PE because of his "Establishment" views (e.g., pro-immigration, global trade agreements, etc.), but Democrats Hillary Clinton (close to Wall Street and corporate America) and Joe Biden are also acceptable to the PE, the latter because of his support for the "new world order." In his May 2014 message to the 995 members of the Air Force Academy graduating class, Vice President Biden said "I believe we and mainly you have an incredible opportunity to lead in shaping a new world order for the twenty-first century in a way consistent with American interests and common interests.

The point is that in election after election, the people think they have a choice, but they really don't.

In 1912, Woodrow Wilson said: "… We have come to be … one of the most completely controlled and dominated governments in the civilized world—no longer a government of conviction and the vote of the majority, but a government by the opinion and duress of small groups of dominant men. …" The PE have been in control ever since and are currently manipulating events to bring about a world currency. In the June 6, 2008, *Asia Times,* Hossain Askari and Nourredine Krichene wrote "Time Overdue for a World Currency," in which they stated: "The world economy is suffering from high inflation stemming from overly expansionary policy in the United States." Their proposed solution—a world currency! Just what the PE wants.

# Chapter 10

# Conspiracy

For quite some time, a friend has expressed his frustration with many people he had contacted regarding the existence of a conspiracy to bring about a world government. These skeptics simply would not listen to his arguments. This isn't hard to believe given that people like Rush Limbaugh have derided conspiracy theorists as being "kooks."

Like many skeptics, he believes that if there is some massive conspiracy taking place, one of the conspirators at some time over many decades would have come forth and revealed what was happening. Well, they have! But Rush either doesn't know it, or is unwilling to admit it.

One skeptic, online, criticized my position by quoting from my books evidence that was circumstantial. However, Special Judge Advocate John A. Bingham said in *The Trial of the Conspirators for the Assassination of President Lincoln* in 1865 that

> In *United States vs Cole et al.*, Mr. Justice McLean says: "A conspiracy is rarely, if ever, proved by positive testimony." Rather, Judge Bingham noted that Justice McLean indicated that conspirators' guilt most often "can be proved only by circumstantial evidence." It is said by some writers on evidence that such circumstances are stronger than positive proof. A witness swearing

positively may misapprehend the facts or swear falsely, but that circumstances cannot lie!

History is full of conspiracies, with rulers of nations plotting to overthrow other rulers. However, in terms of a world government conspiracy, I thought it would be useful to readers of NewsWith-Views, who are themselves trying to convince skeptics, if I presented a chapter in the form of a dialogue between myself and a skeptic (let's call him "Jim"] in order to show how others might be persuaded. The chapter begins as follows:

• • • • •

I told Jim that gold and diamond magnate Cecil Rhodes had formed the secret Society of the Elect in 1891 and had said, "Fancy the charm to young America ... to share in a scheme to take the government of the whole world!"

Jim replied, "Okay, so you found that Cecil Rhodes formed a secret society. That doesn't mean that it actually became a controlling power. Before you are going to get me or anyone else to believe in this conspiracy stuff, you're going to have to come up with someone like a U.S. president confirming it. And I don't mean a right-winger, either. I mean someone like Woodrow Wilson, a liberal intellectual Democrat."

I then told Jim that President Wilson in his *The New Freedom*, published the first year of his presidency (1913), had written:

> Since I entered politics, I have chiefly had men's views confided
> to me privately. Some of the biggest men in the United States, in
> the field of commerce and manufacturing, are afraid of some-
> body, are afraid of something. They know that there is a power
> somewhere so organized, so subtle, so watchful, so interlockerd,
> so complete, so pervasive, that they had better not speak above

their breath when they speak in condemnation of it. ... We have been dreading all along the time when the combined power of high finance would be greater than the power of the government. ... We have come to be one of the worst ruled, one of the most completely controlled and dominated, governments in the civilized world—no longer a government of free opinion, no longer a government by conviction and the vote of the majority, but a government by the opinion and duress of small groups of dominant men."

I also told Jim that relevant to President Wilson's establishment of the Federal Reserve in 1913, Frank Vanderlip (president of Rockefeller's National City Bank) revealed in *The Saturday Evening Post* (February 9, 1935) that he "was as secretive—indeed, as furtive— as any conspirator" in the execution of their plans to form that body.

Skeptic Jim retorted, "Oh, no! I've heard these conspiracy theories about American bankers before. If you're going to say anything about bankers or financiers like J. P. Morgan being involved in this, you better come up with confirmation by another high-ranking, respected American official, just as before," he advised.

Responding to Jim, I told him that in the early years of President Franklin Roosevelt's administration, right after FDR had talked with Jack Morgan (J. P. Morgan' son), the president wrote to Col. Edward M. House (President Wilson's chief advisor) on November 21, 1933, explaining that "The real truth of the matter is, as you and I know, that a financial element in the larger centers has owned government ever since the days of Andrew Jackson. ..."

Jim seemed surprised that a president like FDR would actually say something that bold, and he replied: "Look, this is all very interesting, but it's still people like FDR and Woodrow Wilson talking about what others are doing. You're going to have to show me someone admitting that he, himself, was personally carrying out

Cecil Rhodes' plan decades after Rhodes' death for me to believe that this is more than just Rhodes' pipe dream."

As someone interested in history, I was aware of the works of the famous historian Arnold Toynbee, who was an acknowledged member of Cecil Rhodes' Association of Helpers. Therefore, I showed Jim a speech Toynbee had delivered in Copenhagen in June 1931 (forty years after Rhodes formed his secret society "to take the government of the whole world") to the Institute for the Study of International Affairs, in which he revealed:

> We are at present working discreetly with all our might to wrest this mysterious force called sovereignty out of the clutches of the local nation states of the world. All the time we are denying with our lips what we are doing with our hands, because to impugn the sovereignty of the local nation states of the world is still a heresy for which a statesman or publicist can perhaps not quite be burned at the stake but certainly be ostracized or discredited.

Still skeptical, though, Jim downplayed my discovery by saying, "But Arnold Toynbee is dead, and so are J. P. Morgan and all those other bankers back then. Besides, we're in a global economy today. You'll have to find something linking Morgan to international bankers today if your theory is going to have any credibility."

I knew that Morgan was largely responsible for the establishment of the Bank for International Settlements (BIS) under the Hague Agreement of 1930. The BIS became the central bank for all the world's central banks. And Bill Clinton's Georgetown University mentor, Prof. Carroll Quigley, had written in *Tragedy and Hope* (1966) that its aim was

> to create a world system of financial control in private hands able to dominate the political system of each country and the

economy of the world as a whole. The system was to be controlled in a feudalist fashion by the central banks of the world acting in concert, by secret agreements arrived at in frequent meetings and conferences. The apex of the system was to be the Bank for International Settlements in Basel, Switzerland, a private bank owned and controlled by the world's central banks which were themselves private corporations. Each central bank sought to dominate its government by its ability to control Treasury loans, to manipulate foreign exchanges, to influence the level of economic activity in the country, and to influence cooperative politicians by subsequent economic rewards in the business world.

Jim wanted to see the linkage between Morgan's influence back then (the early twentieth century) and today, so I showed Jim three recent sources that demonstrated the influence and power of the BIS (established largely because of Morgan) in relatively recent times. In 1995, not only did former *Forbes* magazine staff reporter Steven Solomon author *The Confidence Game: How Unelected Central Bankers Are Governing the Changed World*

### The Bank for International Settlements

In George Orwell's *1984*, a description of the future under "Big Brother" is given as "a boot stamping on a human face — forever." Could the "boot" be the new eighteen-story Bank for International Settlements (BIS) which was completed in Basel, Switzerland, in 1977 in the shape of a boot (see picture above), and became known as the "Tower of Basel"? The BIS was originally founded by J. P. Morgan and Co. and others under the Hague Agreement of 1930 as *the* bank for central banks (e.g., U.S. Federal Reserve, German Bundesbank, Bank of Japan, etc.) around the world and exempt from taxation.

*Economy* (including the BIS), but *The New York Times* also provided a statement. On August 5, 1995, the newspaper printed an article by Keith Bradsher, in which he wrote:

> In a small Swiss city sits an international organization so obscure and secretive ... control of the institution, the Bank for International Settlements, lies with some of the world's most powerful and least visible men: the heads of 32 central banks, officials able to shift billions of dollars and alter the course of economies at the stroke of a pen.

Also, on June 28, 1998, *The Washington Post* published an article about the BIS titled: "At secret meetings in Switzerland, 13 people shape the World's Economy," which described these individuals as "this economic cabal ... this secretive group ... the financial barons who control the world's supply of money."

Further evidence of the power of money was provided on ABC Television's July 1, 1998, "Nightline" program in which host Ted Koppel's guest, David Turecamo, revealed that "... power in the world is no longer with politicians. They can be toppled with the click of a mouse ... [moving] huge amounts of money into and out of markets in a nanosecond. ... Money knows no allegiance. There is no patriotism."

I thought Jim would be impressed with all of this. However, while he expressed some interest, he was still reluctant to believe a power elite was manipulationg world events.

Regarding what I had just told him, Jim replied: "Okay, so you've found powerful people who wanted to do something. What specific evidence do you have that any of Cecil Rhodes' secret society was working with influential Americans to pursue their desired goals?"

To provide Jim with such evidence, I looked at the *Journals and Letters of Reginald, Viscount Esher,* one of Cecil Rhodes' executive committee members. Under August 3, 1917, I found this entry: "No American is likely to be killed before November. This is unfortunate, as [President] Wilson may require to be steadied before then and only the death of young Americans can ensure him stability." Esher followed this on August 11 with the statement:

> Mr. Henry Morgenthau asked me to call on him. ... [He] was one of the principal supporters of President Wilson in the campaign for the Presidency, and he possesses the friendship and confidence of the president. ... They are ready to sacrifice the lives of American citizens. ... Mr. Morgenthau realizes the importance upon the morale of the French army and the French people of cementing the Alliance by shedding American blood at the earliest possible moment. If many lives have to be sacrificed, the influence upon the American people can only be beneficent.

Knowing that after the First World War, President Wilson's chief advisor, Colonel House, had been instrumental in founding the Council on Foreign Relations (CFR), another of the conspiracy buffs' targets, I had received pages from a rare, unpublished copy of his diaries and found an extraordinary revelation. An entry by Colonel House in January 1919 said:

> I had a heart to heart talk with Clemenceau [Premier of France] about Bolshevism in Russia and its westward march. I made him confess that military intervention was impossible. ... Later in the afternoon when Orlando [Premier of Italy] called, I gave him very much the same kind of talk, and he too, agreed with my conclusions. I am trying, and have partially succeeded, to frighten not only the president [Wilson] but the English, French and Italians regarding what might be termed "the Russian peril." ... I would not confess that military intervention was

an impossibility, because I believe that it could be successfully accomplished if gone about properly. A voluntary and a mercenary army of very small proportions, equipped with artillery and tanks, would in my opinion do the work.

House here admitted that the spread of the Bolshevik Revolution could have been stopped, but he deliberately misled world leaders, including President Wilson to whom he was chief advisor, to prevent them from stopping it! I thought of the millions of people who were eventually slaughtered by the Bolsheviks, and the costly arms race, and the communists' threat of nuclear holocaust hanging over our heads the past almost seventy years, and asked myself why Colonel House had done this. Then I remembered that he had anonymously authored *Philip Dru: Administrator* in 1912 promoting "socialism as dreamed of by Karl Marx." The goal was to use Marx's "Hegelian" (actually developed by Jacob Boehme in the early 1600s) dialectic of Bolshevik communism as the antithesis to the thesis of Western capitalism, with a resulting synthesis into a world socialist government. This made a great deal of sense given what CFR member Lincoln Bloomfield wrote in his 1962 study, "A World Effectively Controlled by the United Nations," in which he revealed that "… if the communist dynamic was greatly abated, the West might lose whatever incentive it had for world government."

I knew that before I even mentioned the CFR to Jim, I had to have at least two respected scholars confirming that the CFR was a "front" for the power elite. First, I referred to noted Harvard University historian and Kennedy administration advisor Arthur Schlesinger, Jr.'s book *A Thousand Days* (1965) in which he indicated that the CFR (as well as the Rockefeller, Ford, and Carnegie Foundations) was a "front organization" for the power elite. Secondly, I referred to Prof. Carroll Quigley's book *Tragedy and Hope* (1966), in which he also said that the CFR was a "front" for the power elite. Quigley further remarked: "I know of the operations of this network [of power] ... and was permitted for two years, in the early 1960s, to examine its papers and secret records. I have no aversion to it. ... "

Professor Quigley also related that the power elite

expected that they would be able to control both political parties equally. Indeed, some of them intended to contribute to both and allow an alternation of the two parties in public office in order to conceal their own influence, inhibit any exhibition of independence by politicians, and allow the electorate to believe that they were exercising their own free choice.

This is similar to what FDR's son-in-law, Curtis Dall (a member of the New York Stock Exchange), wrote in *FDR: My Exploited Father-In-Law,* as he revealed that

carefully screened leading "actors" are picked well in advance of election day by a small group, picked for both major parties. ... For a long time I felt that FDR had developed many thoughts and ideas that were his own to benefit this country, the U.S.A. But he didn't. Most of his thoughts, his political "ammunition," as it were, was carefully manufactured for him in advance by the CFR-One-World Money group.

Dall went on to explain that the October 1927 stock market crash

was the calculated "shearing" of the public by the World-Money powers, triggered by the planned sudden shortage of the supply of call money in the New York money market. He was supported in this contention by Congressman Louis McFadden, chairman of the House Committee on Banking and Currency, who had at least two assassination attempts made upon his life. In Congress in 1934, McFadden said that the beginning of the

Great Depression in 1929 "was not accidental. It was a carefully contrived occurrence. ... The international bankers sought to bring about a condition of despair here so they might emerge as rulers of us all."

Confirming the existence of a power elite, President Richard Nixon in *The Real War* (1980) wrote:

The nation's immediate problem is that while the common man fights America's wars, the intellectual elite sets its agenda. Today, whether the West lives or dies is in the hands of its new power elite: those who set the terms of public debate, who manipulate the symbols, who decide whether nations or leaders will be depicted on 100 million television sets as "good" or "bad." This power elite sets the limits of the possible for Presidents and Congress. It molds the impressions that move the nation, or that mire it.

Further confirmation also comes from *The Conservators* (1983) by President Franklin Roosevelt's son, Elliot Roosevelt, who wrote that "there are within our world perhaps only a dozen organizations which shape the courses of our various destinies as rigidly as the regularly constituted governments ... this unofficial council of the elite, the crème de la crème of global planners."

When skeptic Jim heard this, the expression on his face became extremely serious. He was still reluctant to believe that there existed a power elite manipulating events, but he was at least willing to tolerate the belief that it was a possibility. In a very deliberate tone, he said, "All right, for this theory of yours to pan out, you still have to demonstrate that manipulation not only occurred at the highest levels and included the electorate, but that it also reached down to affect the masses of people beyond the electorate as well."

I knew that part of Cecil Rhodes' plan was to penetrate and control the areas of politics, economics, education, and journalism. And I knew that in the *Congressional Record* (February 19, 1917) as well as other places, there was testimony regarding interests of J. P. Morgan buying control of newspapers so that they could be properly "edited." The revolutionary Antonio Gramsci had written that to control a society, one had to first capture the culture, and in 1928 when CFR member William Paley started CBS, Paley hired Sigmund Freud's nephew, Edward Bernays, as his chief advisor. In that same year, Bernays authored *Propaganda,* in which he revealed:

> Those who manipulate the organized habits and opinions of the masses constitute an invisible government which is the true ruling power of the country. ... It remains a fact that in almost every act of our lives, whether in the sphere of politics or business, in our social conduct or our ethical thinking, we are dominated by the relatively small number of persons. ... It is they who pull the wires which control the public mind, who harness old social forces and contrive new ways to bind and guide the world. ... As civilization has become more complex, and as the need for invisible government has been increasingly demonstrated, the technical means have been invented and developed by which opinion may be regimented."

I informed Jim of these things and also told him that similar to what Bernays had written, scholar Christopher Simpson in *Science and Coercion: Communication Research and Psychological Warfare, 1945-1960* wrote that

> Harold Lasswell and Walter Lippmann advocated ... a particular social order in the United States and the world in which forceful elites necessarily ruled in the interest of their vision

of the greater good. U.S-style consumer democracy was simply a relatively benign system for engineering mass consent for the elite's authority. ... Harold Lasswell had the ear of [Rockefeller] Foundation administrator John Marshall. ... The elite of U.S. society ["those who have money to support research," as Lasswell bluntly put it] should systematically manipulate mass sentiment.

Supporting Lasswell's and Lippmann's view, author Aldous Huxley in *The Devils of Loudun* wrote of how the masses could be conditioned, explaining:

> If exposed long enough to the tomtoms and singing, every one of our philosophers would end by capering and howling with the savages. ... Assemble a mob of men and women previously conditioned by a daily reading of newspapers; treat them to amplified band music, bright lights ... and in next to no time you can reduce them to a state of almost mindless subhumanity. Never before have so few been in a position to make fools, maniacs, or criminals of so many.

I told Jim this and that in George Orwell's book, *1984*, when the hero Winston tells Big Brother's agent, O'Brien, that people will never accept his planned, controlled future society, O'Brien knowingly responds, "Suppose that we quicken the tempo of human life," so that people have less time to analyze what is happening to them and resist it. Orwell died only a few months after writing this book, just as Prof. Carroll Quigley died not too long after an article was printed in *The Washington Post* about him, titled "The Professor Who Knew Too Much."

When I told Jim that I had actually gotten a copy of the taped interview of *The Washington Post* reporter and Professor Quigley, Jim knew that I was very serious about the subject, and he was even beginning to believe that there was a power elite behind the scenes manipulating events and people's lives. So, he puzzlingly asked, "What do these people want? I mean, I know they want power and control, but for what purpose? What's their ultimate design for the world?"

I replied that I believe they intend to synthesize Western capitalism and Eastern communism into a world socialist government.

"How did you come to that conclusion?" Jim inquired.

I told him about what I had come across earlier in Colonel House's diaries along with the Lincoln Bloomfield quote, and then I said that when I heard President George H. W. Bush use the term, "new world order," I recalled that the famous Fabian socialist H. G. Wells had written a book by that same title in 1939. In the book, he projected just such a synthesis and also said "countless people … will hate the new world order … and will die protesting against.

"Aw, c'mon," Jim replied with disbelief. "You mean to tell me that Wells predicted 'the new word order,' using those exact words, over seventy years ago?"

I found Jim's incredulity amusing, given all that I had already provided him in the way of documentation concerning the power elite. "Actually," I said, "Wells' *The New World Order* was the last of his efforts in this regard, as he had earlier written *The Open Conspiracy: Blue Prints For a World Revolution* in 1928, and *The Shape of Things To Come* in 1933. In this 1933 book, Wells had actually predicted a Second World War would begin around 1940 over a German-Polish dispute, and that the 'modern world-state' (new world order) would begin around forty years from then and come out of something that would occur in Basra, Iraq. He said that although world government 'had been plainly coming for years, although it had been endlessly feared and murmured against, it found no opposition prepared anywhere.' Wells had even written a book in 1901 titled *Anticipations,* in which he acknowledged that the men of the new world order 'will not be squeamish either in facing or inflicting death. ... They will have an ideal that will make killing worth the while.'"

This talk about "inflicting death" and "killing" was upsetting to Jim, who tried to dismiss it by saying, "Look, Orwell's Big Brother wound up killing a lot of people, too, but that's just fiction. No one really intends to kill a lot of people in the future in order to establish some kind of socialist utopia."

I said, "Hey, you don't have to believe me. Just look at the statements of leading Fabians like George Bernard Shaw and Bertrand Russell themselves. In *The Intelligent Woman's Guide to Socialism and Capitalism*, Shaw proposed that under socialism 'you would be forcibly fed, clothed, lodged, taught, and employed whether you liked it or not. If it were discovered that you had not character and industry enough to be worth all this trouble, you might possibly be executed in a kindly manner.'

"And Bertrand Russell in *The Impact of Science on Society* related:

'I think the subject which will be of most importance politically is mass psychology ... verses set to music and repeatedly intoned are very effective. ... Although this science will be diligently studied, it will be rigidly confined to the governing class. The populace will not be allowed to know how its convictions were generated. ... Population can be kept from increasing. ... Perhaps bacteriological war may prove effective. If a Black Death could be spread throughout the world once in every generation survivors could procreate freely without making the world too full. ... A scientific world society cannot be stable unless there is a (socialist) world government. ..."'

"OK," Jim blurted out, "so some wild socialists rant about what they might do in the future if they ever get a world socialist government. That still doesn't mean a decade by decade plan was being successfully carried out to get to that point. For example, you talked about Lord Esher and Henry Morgenthau,Sr. wanting to get America into World War I. Did any Fabian beside Wells or any leading American official even have any foreknowledge of America's entry into World War II?

Jim was right, of course. A couple of people promoting America's entry into the First World War could be seen as an isolated event. Therefore, I searched for Fabian possible foreknowledge about Pearl Harbor, and found that on December 5, 1941, Sir Julian Huxley (a Fabian) said that he hoped America and Japan would be at war "next week." The Japanese attack on Pearl Harbor occurred just two days later on Sunday, the first day of the "next week."

As for foreknowledge by an American official, I found that President Roosevelt's secretary of war, Henry Stimson (a founder of the Council on Foreign Relations and member of Skull & Bones), had written the following in his diary for November 25, 1941: "President Roosevelt brought up the event that we are likely to be attacked perhaps [as soon as] next Monday, for the Japanese are notorious for making an attack without warning, and the question was how we should maneuver them into the position of firing the first shot."

Jim seemed staggered by my revelation of what Secretary of War Stimson had written, and he fell back to the standard position of retreat for those who ridicule conspiracy theories. He laughingly remarked: "The next thing you're going to tell me is that after the Second World War, there were all these communist sympathizers in our government. That's just McCarthyism."

"Look, Jim," I replied, "you don't have to take my word for any of this. About McCarthy and the communists, would you take the word of communists themselves? And would you trust the accuracy of former *Washington Post* reporter Carl Bernstein?"

Remembering that Bernstein along with Bob Woodard had cracked the "Watergate" case, Jim said he'd be willing to believe such sources. I then told him that in Bernstein's book, *Loyalties: A Son's Memoir,* his father (who along with Carl's mother had been members of the of the Communist Party in America) told Carl:

> You're going to prove McCarthy right, because all he was saying was that the system was loaded with communists. And he was right. You've got to take a big hard look at what you're doing. Because the whole fight against him was that people weren't communists. ... I'm worried about the kind of book you're going to write and about cleaning up McCarthy. The problem is that everybody said he was a liar; you're saying he was right. ... I agree that the Party was a force in the country.

I went on to tell Jim that during the 1950s at the same time the McCarthy controversy was growing, an organization called World Association of Parliamentarians for World Government actually prepared a map showing what foreign troops would police the various nations of the world when the world government came into existence. Jim didn't think this was very important until I informed him that according to this map, U.S. troops would be policing in Yugoslavia, and Russian troops would be policing in the southern and southeastern U.S. To Jim, this was somewhat alarming because he knew that in 1995 U.S. troops had been sent to Yugoslavia, and he knew that Russian troops had been at Fort Riley (Kansas) and Fort Polk (Louisiana), and that a Russian policeman had helped arrest someone in western North Carolina. I told Jim also to keep in mind that this map was distributed at the 1959 United World Federalists convention, which had Mr. (later U.S. Senator) and Mrs. Alan Cranston as member sponsors.

Jim asked to see the map, and when I showed it to him, he noticed that when the world government comes into existence, American troops are also supposed to be policing Australia. He looked up from the map quickly and told me that just that morning he had received a fax from friends in Australia telling him that near the end of July 1996, a large number of U.S. Marines were permanently stationed in Australia, with three thousand supposedly coming and going for training. He also indicated that his friends had sent him information regarding the increasing uneasiness in that nation concerning the possible disarming of citizens. One Australian newspaper editorialized that the pressure for this disarmament "must be from outside Australia."

I told Jim that would fit with the statement in "Our Global Neighborhood," the report of the Commission on Global Governance, that "We strongly endorse community initiatives ... to encourage the disarming of citizens." The work of the commission was endorsed by U.N. Secretary-General Boutros Boutros-Ghali. It received funding from governments such as those of the Netherlands, Sweden, India, Switzerland, and others, and from foundations such as the MacArthur Foundation and the Ford Foundation, as well as from the Carnegie Corporation. Its report was published by Oxford University Press in 1995.

I also reminded Jim that prior to any massive slaughter of people in various countries such as the Soviet Union, Nazi Germany, communist China, Guatemala, Uganda, Colombia, or Ottoman Turkey over the years, there were "gun control" laws enacted. Jim contested that our government wouldn't try to disarm its citizens, but I informed him that the attitude of the government regarding the Second Amendment to the Constitution could allow them to move in that direction. I then showed him a letter from the U.S. Department of Justice dated February 20, 1997, which stated: "The current state of federal law does not recognize that the Second Amendment protects the right of private citizens to possess firearms of any type. Instead, the Second Amendment is deemed to be a collective right belonging to the state, not to an individual." I then went on to inform Jim that there had been documents prepared by the administration of President Kennedy calling for the disarmament of national armies down to the point where no country "would have the military power to challenge the progressively strengthened U.N. Peace Force."

Because I knew that Jim was becoming interested in how Cecil Rhodes' plan had tracked through the decades, I mentioned to him that President Kennedy had at least a dozen Rhodes scholars in his administration. One Rhodes scholar whom I stressed in particular was Richard N. Gardner, who was a high-ranking State Department official from 1961 to 1965. The reason I emphasized Gardner to Jim was that Gardner later wrote an article in the CFR's journal *Foreign Affairs* (April 1974) stating that "the 'house of world order' will have to be built from the bottom up, rather than from the top down, ... but an end run around national sovereignty, eroding it piece by piece, will accomplish much more than the old-fashioned frontal assault."

Gardner in the article further revealed that "we will be seeking new rules in the GATT to cover a whole range of hitherto unregulated nontariff barriers. These will subject countries to an unprecedented degree of international surveillance over up to now sacrosanct 'domestic' policies."

Gardner later would be an advisor on U.N. matters to the Clinton presidential campaign. And after Bill Clinton's election in 1992, Gardner would be appointed ambassador to Spain, from which the new head of NATO, the Marxist/socialist Javier Solana, would come with the support of the Clinton administration.

When the still skeptical Jim heard the word "Marxist," an exasperated look came upon his face, and he sighed, "Here we go with the commies again."

I quickly responded: "Jim, you have got to stop having these kneejerk reactions. I am not saying this is all a commie plot, but you do yourself a disservice if you do not take seriously the words of leading political figures in this country."

"What are you talking about?" Jim replied. Because I knew that the Trilateral Commission was another of the conspiracy buffs' targets, I informed Jim that before Zbigniew Brzezenski (ZB) had become the first director of David Rockefeller's Trilateral Commission in the early 1970s, ZB had written *Between Two Ages* (1970), in which he proclaimed:

> Marxism is simultaneously a victory of the external, active man over the inner, passive man and a victory of reason over belief ... [and] the fiction of [national] sovereignty ... is clearly no longer compatible with reality. ... In the technetronic society the trend seems to be toward ... effectively exploiting the latest communication techniques to manipulate emotions and control reason. ... Human beings become increasingly manipulable and malleable."

Regarding communications in the "technetronic society," I asked Jim if he knew that AT&T with its company NCR (National Cash Register) had a full-page ad in *USA Today* on September 17, 1992, highlighting the Chinese philosophic yin-yang symbol. Then I asked if he knew about AT&T's formation of Lucent Technologies in 1996 with a red circle for a logo. I also asked Jim, "Isn't Lucent's new 'network operating and programming environment' called 'Inferno'? And doesn't a Lucent publicity release quote from Dante's *The Inferno* (about Hell and Lucifer)? And didn't Lucent materials state that 'Inferno (Internet/computer) applications are written in a new language called "Limbo" which was designed specifically for the Inferno environment' (Limbo is a region bordering on Hell)? And aren't the 'communications protocols' in Lucent's software called 'styx' (in mythology, the river Styx encircles Hades or Hell)? And didn't Lucent sign a lease for 40,000 square feet at 666 Fifth Avenue in New York?" I asked Jim if he thought all of this was just a meaningless coincidence.

I then reminded Jim that after ZB had written the statement quoted above from his book, *Between Two Ages,* he was made President Jimmy Carter's national security advisor. And at the first

State of the World Forum (September 27–October 1, 1995) chaired by former Soviet leader Mikhail Gorbachev, Brzezinski declared: "We cannot leap into world government through one quick step. A consensual global system requires a process. ... The precondition for eventual and genuine globalization is progressive regionalization because by that we move toward larger, more stable, more cooperative units." Then, to persuade Jim with evidence from a liberal source that there really is a power elite running the world, I quoted from George Cothran's article, "Global Chic: Gorby's Bash by the Bay," which was printed in *The Washington Post* (September 4, 1995) just three days before the State of the World Forum began. Cothran said that "maybe challenging the powers-that-be isn't Gorbachev's main objective. Rather than disrupting the hidebound elites that run the world, the former Soviet president seems more intent on rejoining their exclusive club."

As confirmation that the Trilateral Commission was part of the power elite's overall scheme. I told Jim to read Sen. Barry Goldwater's autobiography, *With No Apologies,* in which the former U.S. senator explained:

> In my view the Trilateral Commission represents a skillful, coordinated effort to seize control and consolidate the four centers of power—political, monetary, intellectual, and ecclesiastical. All this is to be done in the interest of creating a more peaceful, more productive world community. What the Trilateralists truly intend is the creation of a worldwide economic power superior to the political governments of the nation-states involved. They believe the abundant materialism they propose to create will overwhelm existing differences. As managers and creators of the system, they will rule the future.

I told Jim to note particularly that Senator Goldwater had mentioned "ecclesiastical" power in addition to political, monetary, and intellectual power. That is because the power elite (PE) want everything under their control, and that means there must be not only a world economy managed by a world government, but a one-world religion, too.

Skeptical as always, Jim asked if any religious leaders had fore-warned of the plans of the PE, and I replied that as a matter of fact, even before H. G. Wells had written his *Open Conspiracy* and *The New World Order* books, Pope Benedict XV on July 20, 1920, had warned:

> The coming of a world state is longed for, by all the worst and most distorted elements. This state, based on the principles of absolute equality of men and a community of possessions, would banish all national loyalties. In it no acknowledgment would be made of the authority of a father over his children, or of God over human society. If these ideas are put into practice, there will inevitably follow a reign of unheard-of terror.

Jim shivered at this thought, and I asked him if he knew about Martin Scorsese's blasphemous film, *The Last Temptation of Christ*. Jim said he had heard about it, so I told him it was based on the book by the same title by Nikos Kazantzakis, a famous philosophical syncretist who believed in synthesizing opposing ideas, trends, and realities. I then informed Jim that in Marilyn Ferguson's *The Aquarian Conspiracy* (1980), she said Kazantzakis in 1927 envisioned a union of individuals "who might create for earth a brain and heart, comrades he might signal 'with a password, like conspirators.'"

I went on to tell Jim that John Dewey, the "Father of Progressive Education," had promoted a one-world religion in his book, *A Common Faith*, published the year after his co-authored *Humanist Manifesto* (1933) and two years after he was made honorary president of the National Education Association (NEA) in 1932.

Not many years after this, Dewey became the president of the League for Industrial Democracy, formerly titled the Intercollegiate Socialist Society.

Since "education" played a major part in the PE's plans, I pointed out to Jim that leading "progressive" educators in 1915 formed the Educational Trust to try to direct the future of American education. One of the members of the Trust was George Strayer, who in 1918 became president of the NEA, and one principal recalled "Strayer's Law" for dealing with disloyal subordinates was "Give 'em the ax." Leading officials of the NEA for decades supported "world government," using that specific term. And in the late 1940s, the NEA helped to found the National Training Laboratories (NTL), which in 1962 published *Issues In (Human Relations) Training*. The NEA has supported "human relations" or "sensitivity training" for years, and in this NTL publication one reads that human relations or sensitivity training "fits into a context of institutional influence procedures which includes coercive persuasion in the form of thought reform or brainwashing."

Jim had a rather traditional education as a child, and it was difficult for him to believe that anybody associated with the NEA would try to change people's traditional values. I told him, however, that NEA president Catherine Barrett in the early 1970s admitted that by the year 2000, basic skills would be drastically reduced in education and, she said, "When this happens—and it's near—the teacher can rise to his true calling. More than a dispenser of information, the teacher will be a conveyor of values, a philosopher. ... We will be agents of change."

I told Jim that the executive director of a National Education Association (NEA) affiliate claimed that Saul Alinsky's *Rules For Radicals* had become the NEA's "bible," and that President Obama and Hillary Clinton had also been interested in Alinsky's theories about community organizing. Jim recognized Alinsky as a revolutionary radical, and I asked him, "Did you know that book by

Alinsky has an acknowledgment to Lucifer at the front?" A look of distress came upon Jim's face, and I further related that in the book, Alinsky argued that the radical organizer

> dedicated to changing the life of a particular community must first rub raw the resentments of the people of the community; fan the latent hostilities of many of the people to the point of overt expression. ... An organizer must stir up dissatisfaction and discontent. ... He knows that all values are relative, ... truth to him is relative and changing.

I told Jim that some supporters of the one-world conspiracy have announced that we are moving from the Piscean Age (Christian age of moral absolutes) to the Aquarian Age in which truth is relative (humanistic moral relativism based upon situation ethics). Then I related that Marilyn Ferguson in her book, *The Aquarian Conspiracy* (1980), promoting this conspiracy, wrote:

> There are legions of conspirators ... [who] are linked. ... They have coalesced into small groups in every town and institution. ... They amplify the activities of the conspiracy by networking and pamphleteering. ... Of the Aquarian conspirators surveyed, more were involved in education than any other single category of work.

More recently, former Vatican official Malachi Martin stated in *The New American* (June 9, 1997):

> The Pope is surrounded by men in clerical garb who do not possess the Catholic faith; they are working with foundations, non-governmental organizations, international groups, finan-cial institutions, governments, academia, and other agencies to bring a new world order into existence. ... The governments of

the world will be directed by those who have climbed their way into the capstone. ... They are a new type of human being, an internationalist who seeks to control mankind. ... Collectively, they intend to use religion, governments, and anything they find useful to impose their will. It is my opinion, for instance, that the U.S.S.R. did not disintegrate naturally but was ordered to collapse. Gorbachev was told to vacate his power base, and also to inform other leaders of the Soviet bloc nations to do likewise.

Those orders came from the capstone. ... In its [new world order] completely planned form, there will be a total globalization of money, and the flow of capital and capital goods will be managed from a single, centrally directed entity such as the Bank for International Settlements in Switzerland. Any nation that does not submit to the new globalized system will perish. In addition, there will be an expanded United Nations which will spread its new ethical structure, already championed by Mikhail Gorbachev and Maurice Strong. This will replace the Ten Commandments and become the basis of a new universal and godless religion.

"Jim," I said, "don't you see that the last two generations of school children have been pounded by this humanistic philosophy of moral relativism in the public schools? Why do you think H. J. Blackham, a founder of the four million-member International Humanist and Ethical Union, said in the September-October issue of *The Humanist* that if schools teach dependence on one's self, with students deciding for themselves what is right and what is wrong, 'they are more revolutionary than any conspiracy to overthrow the government'?"

"They want to remold society's values," I told Jim, and I pointed out that the motto of the Fabian socialists had been "Remould it nearer to the heart's desire." "Don't you find it interesting," I asked Jim, "that Hillary Clinton on a number of occasions has used the

The Fabian Socialists' window ordered by George Bernard Shaw in 1910.

word, 'remold,' when talking about society and values? And don't forget," I informed Jim, "that *The New Socialist Revolution* was the title of a 1973 book by Michael Lerner, who has been an advisor to Hillary Clinton."

"But how are they going to use education to 'remold' society, and 'remold' it and us into what?" Jim rejoined. I then explained to him that traditional American values emphasize individual rights and responsibilities while socialism emphasizes the group. That is why cooperative learning has played a major role in what has been called outcome-based education. And one of the reasons school-to-work initiatives (Plank 10 of Karl Marx's *Communist Manifesto* provides for a "combination of education with industrial produc-tion") have been promoted is that we are being prepared for a techno-feudal society under a world socialist government.

I asked Jim if he was familiar with the noted author Jack London, and when Jim responded affirmatively, I asked him if he was aware that in London's *The Iron Heel* (1907) the author referred to W. J. Ghent's *Our Benevolent Feudalism* (1902) as "the textbook" the "oligarchs" would use to rule in the future (see relevant article, "The New World Order," by A. M. Rosenthal in *The New York Times,* May 5, 1998, p. A31). Jim had not heard of Ghent, so I informed him that Ghent had been the editor of *The American Fabian,* and that our feudal future was laid out in Ghent's book which described the importance of "group fidelity" and indicated that "the teachings of the schools and colleges, the sermons, the editorials ... and even the plays at the theaters will be skillfully and persuasively molded."

During President George H. W. Bush's administration, he highlighted the term "new world order" along with the term, "points of light," which he connected with service. Jim was familiar with this, but he expressed real surprise when I told him that although I didn't believe that President Bush was an occultist, the only other individual I had found who emphasized the terms "new world order" and "points of light" connected with service was Alice Bailey, who was probably the leading occultist in the first half of the twentieth century and whose works were first published by Lucifer Publishing Company.

Jim spoke up, saying "The new world order was just President George H. W. Bush's expression for more global cooperation, such as U.N. peacekeeping efforts."

I reminded Jim that Mikhail Gorbachev on December 7, 1988, had used the term, "new world order," BEFORE president Bush had used it, and I emphasized that this new "cooperation" could only occur after the alleged demise of the Soviet Union, after which the United States military was greatly downsized and we were therefore forced to rely more and more upon "peacekeeping efforts" under the auspices of the United Nations, headed by Boutros Boutros-Ghali, who was a vice president of Socialist International (as has been Gro Harlem Brundtland, former prime minister of Norway, who was elected director-general of the World Health Organization on January 27, 1998) until his election as U.N. secretary-general. The "old-fashioned frontal assault" (Richard Gardner's term) of trying to use the "communist dynamic" mentioned by Lincoln Bloomfield as a means of facilitating a dialectical "compromise for peace" (synthesis of the U.S. and U.S.S.R. into a world socialist government) was now giving way to Richard Gardner's "end run around national sovereignty," using the alleged demise of the "communist dynamic" to cause the U.S. to believe "peace in our time" (a term mistakenly used by British prime minister Neville Chamberlain after negotiations with Hitler) allowed downsizing our military, thereby forcing our greater reliance upon U.N. "peacekeeping" efforts.

"Don't you remember," I asked Jim, "that in the early 1930s, Communist Party theoretician Dimitry Manuilski stated in Moscow that 'one day we shall start to spread the most theatrical peace movement the world has ever seen. The capitalist countries, stupid and decadent ... will fall into the trap offered by the possibility of making new friends. ... Our day will come in thirty to forty years or so. ... The bourgeoisie must be lulled into a feeling of security'?"

Jim did not remember this, but he did say that he remembered the passage in 1 Thessalonians 5:3 that warns: "For when they shall say, Peace and safety; then sudden destruction shall come upon them. ... " And he did acknowledge that he had always thought the alleged coup attempt against Gorbachev was suspicious, and that Gorbachev's replacement by Boris Yeltsin was also curious. I reminded Jim that Gorbachev then set up the Gorbachev Foundation, which took over the Presidio, a former military base in San Francisco. Jim had likewise been suspicious of the sudden transformation of the Soviet Union as "evil empire" into a sort of partner with which we developed the Soviet-American Exchange

Agreement in 1985, allowing Soviet educators to participate in the development of curricula for some American schools.

I asked Jim if he remembered who signed that agreement for the U.S., and he said that he believed that it was Secretary of State George Shultz. I told Jim that he was correct and asked if he knew that Shultz then became chairman of the board of advisers of the Gorbachev Foundation. I also told Jim that former U.S. Senator Alan Cranston (mentioned earlier as a member sponsor of the 1959 United World Federalists convention at which the world government map was distributed) had become chairman of the board of directors of the Gorbachev Foundation.

I asked Jim, "Do you really think all this harmony and cooperation between the U.S. and the former Soviet Union is just an accident? I am going to give you a tape of Norman Dodd (staff director of the Congressional Special Committee to Investigate Tax-Exempt Foundations) revealing that in the fall of 1953, Ford Foundation president H. Rowan Gaither told Dodd the following:

> Of course, you know that we at the executive level here were, at one time or another, active in either the OSS, the State Department, or the European Economic Administration. During those times, and without exception, we operated under directives issued by the White House. We are continuing to be guided by just such directives. … The substance [of these directives] was to the effect that we should make every effort to so alter life in the United States as to make possible a comfortable merger with the Soviet Union.

"And the Gorbachev Foundation is part of the 'comfortable merger'?" Jim asked. I nodded my head affirmatively and went on to explain the matter even further. "To get an idea of the mentality of these people," I said, "do you remember that Gorby's Foundation sponsored a 'State of the World' Forum?" Jim indicated that he had seen something about it in the news some years ago, so I said, "One of the speakers at the first forum in 1995 was Sam Keen, and he evoked tremendous applause when he stated, 'If we cut the world's population by ninety percent, there won't be enough people left to do ecological damage.' Jim, think about what it would take to cut the world's population by ninety percent."

I also asked Jim to think about what it would take for the former CIA director William Colby (who disappeared some years ago and was found dead) to tell John DeCamp: "Sometimes there are forces too powerful for us to whip them individually, in the time frame that we would like. ... The best we might be able to do sometimes, is to point out the truth and then step aside. That is where I think we are now. For your own personal safety and survival, step aside."

A "comfortable merger" between capitalism and communism into world socialism would require the American society moving to the left. But to cause this movement to occur without arousing too much suspicion, the power elite developed a strategy of promoting radical left extremism so that its own initiatives would not appear to be leftist. In 1968, Random House published James Simon Kunen's *The Strawberry Statement,* in which Kunen tells of an SDS (Students for a Democratic Society) strategy meeting he attended where a student was giving a report about an SDS convention the student had recently attended. The student's report revealed that

> ... men from Business International Roundtables ... tried to buy up a few radicals. These men are the world's industrialists and they convene to decide how our lives are gong to go. They're the left wing of the ruling class. They offered to finance our demonstrations in Chicago. We were also offered ESSO [Rockefeller] money. They want us to make a lot of radical commotion so they can look more in the center as they move more to the left.

Jim exclaimed that he now realized that something ominous was in the works, and that there were powerful forces behind it. I was relieved to see that Jim was finally coming around, and to support what he just indicated, I advised him to look at the comments of the self-described socialist Christopher Hitchens on C-Span television on August 23, 1993. Hitchens had been a friend of Bill Clinton at Oxford University when Clinton was a Rhodes scholar back in the late 1960s, and on this C-Span program, he stated: "It is, of course, the case that there is a ruling class in this country [the U.S.] and that it has allies internationally."

An editorial by James K. Fitzpatrick in the national newspaper *The Wanderer* (November 18, 1993) revealed that

> Clinton told reporters in an interview that [Prof. Carroll] Quigley's work centered on the existence of a permanent shadow government of powerful bankers and businessmen and government officials that controls the agenda of our political life from behind the scenes. Clinton spoke in that interview of coming to the conclusion, while still a young man, that it was necessary for him to gain access to the inner circle of this group in order to become part of the decision-making process that shapes our world.

Jim related that when President Clinton nominated Ruth Bader Ginsburg and Stephen Breyer to the U.S. Supreme Court, Jim felt that it had to be more than a coincidence that they were two of the three CFR members among a total of one hundred fifty U.S. Court of Appeals judges from whom President Clinton was likely to select his nominees. I stressed to Jim that Trilateralist and CFR member Bill Clinton's election to the U.S. presidency was a major step forward in Cecil Rhodes' plan "to take the government of the whole world." Jim was now clicking and excitedly said, "Maybe that is why Clinton could appoint Trilateralist, Skull & Bones member, and former CFR president Winston Lord as a State Department official after Lord had said at a town hall meeting on September 29, 1992: 'To a certain extent, we are going to have to yield some of our sovereignty. ... Under NAFTA ... some Americans are going to be hurt as low-wage jobs are taken away."'

Pleased that Jim now was recognizing what was happening, I wanted to give him further support for his realization that the concept of national sovereignty was under attack by the one-world power elite and their Rhodes scholar agents in the Clinton administration. So I reminded Jim that Strobe Talbott (Trilateralist and former CFR director), whom President Clinton had made number two at the Statement Department, had been Bill Clinton's Rhodes scholar roommate at Oxford University (Secretary of Labor Robert Reich was also there at the same time as a Rhodes scholar), I then gave Jim a copy of Talbott's *Time* magazine article of July 20, 1992, wherein he wrote: "Perhaps national sovereignty wasn't such a great idea after all. ... But it has taken the events of our own wondrous and terrible century to clinch the case for world government."

Jim was steamed at this remark by Talbott, and questioned how anyone so blatantly undermining national sovereignty and promoting world government could be appointed to such a high position in our federal government. I replied, "Are you kidding? Look at who appointed him. Talbott received the World Federalist Association's Norman Cousins Global Governance Award for that article, and the WFA received a letter dated June 22, 1993, from President Clinton on White House stationery congratulating Talbott for receiving the award, and stating: 'Norman Cousins worked for world peace and world government. ... Best wishes for an enjoyable reception and for future success.' The WFA's primary reason for existence is to promote world federal government, and for President Clinton specifically to mention the term 'world government' and wish the WFA 'future success' says it all."

One of the WFA's possible strategies was revealed in its *The Genius of Federation: Why World Federation Is the Answer to Global Problems* (1994), in which one reads:

> Still another approach is to advance step by step toward global governance, using the U.N. ... Let the U.N. establish new agencies such as an International Criminal Court or a U.N. Arms Control and Disarmament Agency. ... National sovereignty would be gradually eroded until it is no longer an issue. Eventually a world federation can be formally adopted with little resistance.

I then asked Jim if he had noticed how deferential the Clinton administration had acted toward the U.N. I pointed out how President Clinton on October 13, 1993, had said they were engaging in a political process regarding Somalia "to see how we can ... do all things the United Nations ordered to do. ... " Vice President Al Gore referred to the Americans killed April 14, 1994, as a result of friendly fire attack while patrolling over Iraq, as "those who died in the service of the United Nations." We also allowed the U.N. to veto our request some years ago to "take out" the surface-to-air missiles that almost cost American pilot Scott O'Grady his life in Bosnia. And about ten years ago concerning the removal of Saddam Hussein as ruler of Iraq, President Clinton on February 5, 1998, had said "that is not what the U.N. authorized us to do."

"Yeah," Jim replied, "I saw part of former British prime minister Margaret Thatcher's December 12, 1997, speech in Washington, where she surprised some people by asserting that 'today's international policy makers' ... short-term goal is to subordinate American and other national sovereignties to multinational authorities; their long-term goal, one suspects, is to establish the U.N. as a kind of embryo world government.'"

Picking up on this, I noted to Jim that just two days after Mrs.

Thatcher made those remarks, then-U.S. Senator Chuck Hagel, just back from the U.N. Global Warming Conference in Kyoto, Japan, appeared on CBS' "Face the Nation," December 14, 1997, and warned:

> The consequences of the actions that are taken, and if in fact we move forward and ratify this Treaty on Global Warming, are about our jobs, our economic future, our economic growth, international competitiveness, and national sovereignty. For example, for the first time in the history of America, we would be allowing a U.N. bureaucracy to come in and administer and enforce shutdowns of industries, businessmen and farmers.

To demonstrate the extent to which President Clinton would have gone to pursue a world government (initially via the U.N.), I asked Jim if he recalled hearing about Army Specialist Michael New, who had refused to wear the U.N. insignia over his American uniform when asked (ultimately by President Clinton) to do so as part of his assignment to Macedonia (formerly part of Yugoslavia). When Jim said he had heard about the controversy on the national news some time ago, I told him that the young soldier had captured the irony of the situation in his statement that "he [Clinton] refused to wear the U.S. military uniform [in the Vietnam War] and was elected President of the United States, but when I refused to sur-render my U.S. Army uniform to wear the uniform of another gov-ernment [the U.N.] he had me court-martialed."

Eager to learn more, Jim said, "OK, that's the type of thing they've been doing in foreign affairs. What about domestic affairs?"

"Well," I told him, "perhaps the best description of what's been going on comes from Anatoliy Golitsyn in *The Perestroika Decep-tion* (1995)." I informed Jim that Golitsyn was a Soviet KGB agent who defected to the U.S., and related that in Christopher Story's (editor) foreword to Golitsyn's book, Story wrote:

Control of the Western mind is to be achieved not only by means of the dishonest use of language, but also through operations to demoralize the West—through corrosive attacks on society's institutions, the active promotion of drug abuse, and the spread of agnosticism, nihilism, permissiveness and coerced attacks on the family in order to destabilize society. Religion and the traditional culture and moral hegemony must first be destroyed, before the revolution can be successful—a message stated unequivocally by the American activist Ellen Willis, who had written that "feminism is not just an issue or a group of issues; it is the cutting edge of a revolution in cultural and moral values. ... The objective of every feminist reform, from legal abortion to the E.R.A. to child-care programs, is to undermine traditional family values ..." [see *The Nation*, November 14, 1981]. ... The strategists assume that with Western society "deconstructed," its leaders will meekly accept and cooperate with the Soviet plan for a "New World Social Order," or World Government.

"In order the have a world socialist government," I told Jim, "each nation must first be moved toward socialism, and to accomplish that, key areas must be 'national'-ized. That's why you hear about national service, a national police force, national education standards like under Common Core, and national health care like Obamacare." I reminded Jim that while leading conservative talk-show gurus like Rush Limbaugh, Sean Hannity, and Glenn Beck were saying President Obama would never be re-elected in 2012 because unemployment was so high, etc., I believed he would be re-elected as part of the power elite's secret Nazi plan because he was moving us toward socialism as a nation (taking over Fannie Mae, Freddie Mac, General Motors, etc.), and the word Nazi means national socialism.

Jim interrupted, saying "And didn't Rhodes scholar Ira Magaziner work with Hillary Clinton both on outcome-based education/

school-to-work proposals and her national health care plan?"

"You're right," I replied, and further supported what Jim had just said by telling him that on C-Span, November 20, 1994, noted economist Milton Friedman, speaking on the fiftieth anniversary reissue of F. A. Hayek's book, *The Road to Serfdom*, explained: "Bill Clinton is a socialist, defined as somebody who believes that the way to achieve good things is to have government do it. You can't think of a more socialist program than the health care program that he tried to get us to adopt."

"If the Clinton administration wasn't moving us toward socialism," I asked Jim, "why do you think they made Mary Jo Bane an assistant secretary of Health and Human Services after she had earlier been quoted in an Associated Press article as remarking: "We really don't know how to raise children. If we want to talk about equality of opportunity for children, then the fact that children are raised in families means there's no equality. It's a dilemma. In order to raise children with equality, we must take them away from families and communally raise them'?"

Jim bemoaned the fact that it seemed government wanted to take over more and more of our lives, and I replied that "the takeover of American life by government" was the very subject that Theodore Forstmann wrote about in *The New York Times* (March 27, 1994). Forstmann described the "takeover" in the following terms:

> In the early 1900s, total spending at the federal, state, and local levels was 10 percent of the national income. By 1950, that figure had risen to 26 percent. Today, it stands at 43 percent and continues to grow. ... For the first time, more Americans are employed by Government—18.7 million—than by manufacturing—18.1 million. ... The United States, unfortunately, is moving toward democratic socialism. ... And the Clinton administration—which sees no task as too small, no dream too large, no

issue too delicate for probing Government hands—has clearly joined the statist camp.

And the current Obama administration has moved the nation even further in that direction with his many executive orders.

At this moment in our conversation, Jim and I were interrupted by a phone call. It was the well-known Associated Press writer Fred Bayles (who has since become a university professor in Boston). He had heard about some of my writings on the New World Order and was calling to get some information. As I explained many of the events leading up to the present, he responded by saying that rather than a conspiracy, perhaps what was occurring was just "an organic evolution" in a rapidly changing technological world. I replied that new communications technology did facilitate increasingly rapid global economic transactions, but the problem was whether a power elite was gaining greater control over our lives and whether they were moving us toward a world socialist government.

I explained to Mr. Bayles that what was happening was not a conspiracy in the usual sense, but that Cecil Rhodes' plan (which was but one element of the conspiracy) provided a means whereby in six decades after its implementation, there would be no need for a conspiracy. The idea was that within that time period several thousand key individuals with "politically correct" worldviews would be in strategically important positions, opening doors for others, so that the movement toward a world socialist government would naturally evolve and progress toward the fulfillment of Rhodes' plan.

I later asked Mr. Bayles if he really thought what happened some years ago relative to Maurice Greenberg, who was chairman of the Federal Reserve Bank of New York at the time, was just "organic" or if there had been a manipulation of events by the power elite. Greenberg was also CEO of AIG (American

International Group), which was incorporated in Delaware on July 9, 1967, with executive offices in New York, NY.

If one looks at the Tax Reform Act of 1986, one finds that the new tax law applied to nearly everyone except

> any controlled foreign corporation which on August 16, 1986, was a member of an affiliated group as defined in section 1504 (a) of the (Internal Revenue Code of 1986) without regard to subsection (3) thereof, which had as its common parent a corporation incorporated in Delaware on July 9, 1967, with executive offices in New York, New York. ...

Was this provision that saved AIG millions of dollars just "organic"? And incidentally, former assistant secretary of state Richard Holbrooke on "The Charlie Rose Show" (February 19, 1997) said Greenberg probably knows the new leaders of communist China better than do the people in the U.S. government.

After talking with Mr. Bayles, I told Jim that it seemed as if there was a general unwillingness on the part of most Americans to believe that our national sovereignty is being threatened. "Why," I asked Jim, "won't they believe syndicated columnist Georgie Anne Geyer, who in her *Americans No More* (1996), remarked with chagrin regarding the United States:

> I have never been able to discover another nation in human history, much less a great and powerful one, that literally willed itself out of existence through lethargy and, worst of all, guilt over things it did not even do. ... On October 3, 1965 ... President Lyndon Johnson solemnly signed into law the Immigration Reform Act of 1965. Americans would eventually understand that watershed moment marked the beginning of the end of their sovereignty. Although few people grasped it at the time, the law imposed upon America the idea of a utopian

world without borders—and without borders, if the history of the world is any guide, nations soon come to know only chaos, anarchy, and disintegration?

"And why," I asked, "won't people believe former Citicorp chairman Walter Wriston (CFR member) who, in his *The Twilight of Sovereignty* (1992), explained:

> The world can no longer be understood as a collection of national economies, [but] a single global economy. ... A truly global economy will require concessions of national power and compromises of national sovereignty that seemed impossible a few years ago and which even now we can but partly imagine. ... The global [information] network will be internationalists in their outlook and will approve and encourage the worldwide erosion of traditional sovereignty?

I then reminded Jim that at the Annual Meeting of the International Monetary Fund/World Bank on October 3, 1996, the World Bank president at that time, James Wolfensohn, said that although he thanks God in many ways that the World Bank has not been given world government powers, he nevertheless "wish[ed] ... fifty years ago someone had given us [World Bank] a world government power. ..."

I asked Jim, "Why didn't more people become concerned when Council on Foreign Relations (CFR) member Ted Koppel on ABC's 'Nightline' referred to 'nationalism' as a 'virus'?" As a serious look of concern came upon Jim's face, I showed him an article titled "Winners and Losers in the Informational Age" in the November/December 1996 edition of *Society*. It was written by Ian Angell of the London School of Economics and Political Science (established by Fabian socialists), who proclaimed:

Individuals and companies are setting up large transnational networks that pay absolutely no heed to national boundaries and barriers. ... Those who wrap themselves in the flag can soon expect to be buried in it. ... We can expect massive civil unrest and disorder. ... Governments, like all other organizations, will have to survive economically on the efforts of an elite few—and no nation-state has an automatic right to exist. ... Governments will have no other choice other than to acquiesce to the will of global enterprise. ... As far as global enterprises are concerned, liberal democracy is an artifact ... [which] will soon mutate into an irrelevancy. It will be merely the means of governing the immobile and dependent social workers. That citizens elect their slave masters makes democracy none the less. ... The masses will not win the national selection for dominance of an increasingly elitist world.

Jim said that he guessed that most people, in the back of their minds, probably did believe that there is a power elite threatening our national sovereignty, but they just did not want to face the ultimate implications of that belief. He recounted that during the congressional hearings regarding GATT, Felix Rohatyn testified before the Senate Commerce Committee on November 15, 1994, that powerful international interests had already planned on GATT's passage and had invested accordingly. Jim then said that Rohatyn offered the veiled threat that if GATT did not pass, there would be dire economic consequences.

I said "Jim, I am sure you know that Felix Rohatyn is a Trilateralist, CFR member, and a co-partner with Lazard Brothers. But did you know that the managing director of Lazard Brothers since 1963 (Adam Marris) and before 1963 (Lord Robert Brand) were also head of the Round Table Groups set up by Lord Alfred Milner as part of Cecil Rhodes' plan for world dominion?'

Jim indicated that while he had not known that, he was not

surprised, and he commented: "It is becoming more and more clear to me the control that the power elite exercises. I suppose that is why GATT was rammed through Congress with the support of Republicans like Senator Bob Dole and Speaker Newt Gingrich, and with the support of Democrats including President Bill Clinton, even though polls showed about eighty percent of the American people opposed it."

I agreed with Jim's perception, and thought aloud, "You know, a lot of patriotic militias actually formed due to a perceived threat to our freedoms and national sovereignty, and 'America First' supporters opposed NAFTA and GATT. Have you noticed, Jim, how some of the globalists have been eager to blame things like the Oklahoma City bombing on groups like the patriotic militia? It seems as if they want to associate these groups with illegal violent acts and thereby discredit them, just like they used the name 'McCarthyism' to brand the efforts of anyone trying to expose communists activities in this country."

Jim replied, "Oh, yeah, and they call them right-wing extremists, too."

Concerning Jim's statement that the power elite (PE) likes to refer to those who oppose them as "right-wing extremists," I replied "Yes, but they are going to have a hard time characterizing the leftist Columbia University sociologist C. Wright Mills as a 'right-wing extremist.' And in Mills' *The Power Elite* (1956), he acknowledged:

> There is ... little doubt that the American power elite—which contains, we are told, some of "the greatest organizers in the world"—has ... planned and plotted. ... Certain types of men from each of the dominant institutional areas, more far-sighted than others, have actually promoted the liaison [of the power elite] before it took its truly modern shape. ... The power elite is not all together "surfaced." ... Many higher events that would

reveal the working of the power elite can be withheld from public knowledge under the guise of secrecy. With the wide secrecy covering their operations and decisions, the power elite can mark their intentions, operations and further consolidation. ... New men come into it [the power elite] and assume its existence without question.

"They are also going to have a hard time characterizing the leftist nationally syndicated columnist, Alexander Cockburn, as a 'right-wing extremist.' Cockburn writes for the left-wing magazine. *The Nation,* and in his May 4,1995, column in *The Seattle Times,* he expressed his belief that

> There is, in emerging outline, a world government composed of the International Monetary Fund and the central banks of the leading industrial nations. National sovereignty is being eroded, most recently by the GATT treaty. Libraries are under threat, as now displayed by [President] Clinton's anti-terrorism package. Politics in America are so decayed, so rotted out, that the surprise is not that there are patriotic militias but that there aren't more of them.

I also related that Pulitzer prize-winning writers Don Bartlett and Jim Steele of *The Philadelphia Inquirer* had written a series of articles beginning September 8, 1996, based upon their new book, *America: Who Stole the Dream?* (1996). The series included titles such as "How U.S. Policies Are Costing American Jobs: Washington rules on trade, taxes, immigration and foreign competition—and the growing concentration of corporate power—are moving the nation toward a two-class society"; "Importing Goods, Exporting Jobs: Washington has opened wide the doors of America, the world's most lucrative consumer market, to foreign products, without adequately safeguarding American jobs"; and "Endangered

Label: 'Made in U.S.A.': product after product once made or grown in the United States now comes from abroad. One of the biggest losers in this influx: Small businesses."

Jim nodded his head in agreement and said, "It really helps when you can show that it is not just people on the 'far right' who believe that something is wrong, but that there are also liberals and moderates who see a threat to our freedoms, jobs, and sovereignty."

"To be sure," I replied, "and that is why I quoted Professors Arthur Schlesinger, Jr. and Carroll Quigley saying that the Council on Foreign Relations was a 'front' for the power elite. And that is also why I quote someone like Terry Galanoy, because his former position as director of communications for National Bank-Americard, later Visa, lends credibility to his revealing statements in *Charge It: Inside the Credit Card Conspiracy* (1980), in which he wrote:

> George Orwell's notorious character "Big Brother" will actually turn out to be Big Banker; all-seeing, all-knowing, all-controlling, capable of destroying any resistance. ... Where they're taking you is to a totally different kind of economic society in which you will have little or no privacy, in which your income and everything you own will be under their control. ... You will be a profitable, dependable, fiscally sound, paid-up citizen even if they have to destroy your freedom and even your life to do it.

"Oh my," Jim uttered, "that sounds like they might stop at nothing to get their way."

"You think that is something," I responded, and then said, "You know how some years ago there were airplane and rail accidents, building collapses, and talk about implanting biochip IDs under our skin? Well, I have a tape of a Dr. Lawrence Dunegan describing a speech he heard in Pittsburgh in March 1969 by internationally renowned Dr. Richard L. Day, who has been national medical director of Planned Parenthood from 1965 to 1968 saying some rather startling things relevant to such incidents!

"According to Dr. Lawrence Dunegan, Dr. Richard Day in March 1969 announced that in terms of controlling population, 'Everything is in place, and nobody can stop us now. ... This time we're going to do it right.' Dr. Dunegan then recounted that Dr. Day pronounced the following things were planned: contraceptives would be dispensed at school; abortion would become legal and paid for by tax dollars; homosexuality would be promoted as no longer to be considered abnormal behavior; hard-to-cure diseases would be created; a hard-to-detect means had been developed for inducing heart attacks (assassinations); drug (including alcohol) addiction would be promoted so the unfit would die; euthanasia would be more accepted as the cost of medical care would intentionally be made burdensomely high; divorce would be made easier; ID badges would become more prevalent (eventually implanted under skin, and perhaps a transmitter in dental fillings); all salary payments and purchases would be conducted electronically by computer in one banking system; major world religions (especially Christianity) would have to change into a new world religion, and the churches will help bring it about; more airplane and rail accidents, as well as building and bridge collapses, would occur to create an atmosphere of instability; terrorism would be used to make people demand international controls; and economic interdependence would help lessen national sovereignty, as people would become citizens of the world."

Remember this last concept of "world citizen" has been used by President Obama, and note how many of Dr. Day's other predictions have come true regarding contraceptives, homosexuality, diseases, addictions, euthanasia, building and bridge collapses, electronic payments and purchases, airplane and rail accidents, and terrorist attacks.

After hearing these things, Jim shouted, "Wow, and that was all back in 1969!"

"Oh, it goes back even further than that," I told Jim, continuing: "Back in 1907, Robert Hugh Benson wrote *Lord of the World*, in which he tried to expose what the power elite had planned. And in this amazing book, written ten years BEFORE the Russian Revolution, Benson revealed:

> ... in 1917 ... Communism really began. ... The new order began then. ... [after 1989] the final scheme of Western Free Trade. ... Patriotism has been dying fast. ... With the Release Act in 1998 ... [there were] the ministers of euthanasia. ... [The Lord of the world was] rising out of the heaving dun-coloured waters of American socialism like a vision. ... Free trade all over the world. ... Party must unite with party, country with country, and continent with continent. ... Persecution was coming. ... It involved all the stupendous force of Socialism directed by a brilliant individual. ... America was powerless. ... The appearance of peace has deceived many. ... The press was engineered with extraordinary adroitness. ... The world is one now, not many. Individualism is dead. ... For anyone to say that they believe in God—it is high treason. ... The Humanity Religion was the only one. Man was God. ... No actual point of light breaking the appalling vault of gloom. ...

And because "persecution was coming" and "ministers of euthanasia" were mentioned in *Lord of the World,* I reminded Jim that *The Holy Bible* forewarned us about the Nazis and communists having brothers turn in brothers, about abortions today, and about euthanasia tomorrow. Matthew 10:21 states: "And the brother shall deliver us the brother to death, and the father the child; and the children shall rise up against their parents, and cause them to be put to death." And might Jack Kevorkian be considered a "minister of euthanasia" in 1998?

Jim sat there for a moment in silence and then remarked sadly:

"They have been planning this for a long time, and like H. G. Wells said, as the world government approaches, 'it found no opposition prepared anywhere.' The masses are just going to go along with it for the sake of their jobs or whatever. It looks like T. S. Eliot in 'The Hollow Men' (1925) was right when he said, 'This is the way the world ends. Not with a bang but a whimper.'"

Jim thought for a minute and then asked, "I wonder how the world will end with a 'whimper'?"

I replied that the "whimper" would be a "conditioned response" brought about after psychological probes. For example, I asked Jim if he remembered the case of Terri Schiavo, who was, in effect, dehydrated to death. He said he did remember the case, and I explained she was not the first of the worst such case. However, her lack of being given even food was raised to national attention to see if the public would demand an end to such cruel treatment, or simply "whimper" and allow it to happen. When the public's response was the latter, even though (at the time) Florida governor Jeb Bush could have said that violated Florida's law banning assisted suicide, the power elite knew the public would accept President Obama's so-called "death panels."

I told Jim that the same type of thing happened in the case of little Elian Gonzalez when the public was told he was being returned to the father in communist Cuba. Jeb Bush could have blocked it, saying murdering Cuban communist dictator Fidel Castro had said Elian was not being returned to his father, but to him (Castro). Elian was returned, and the public "whimpered," but did nothing to stop it.

I went on to describe to Jim how the psychological conditioning of the public had been occurring in many aspects of Americans' lives, even via music, and without the public knowing what was happening to them. In the past, music was usually melodic, soft/tender, poetically meaningful, uniquely sounding, not sexually suggestive, intelligent and sincere (such as "It Had To Be

You"). But within the last few decades, music has often become pulsing, loud/rough, repeatedly intoned with a simplistic message, emphasizing the beat, similar sounding, sexually suggestive, showing little intelligence, and with emotional loudness substituting for sincerity. This has conditioned many people to act in a manner reflecting the newer music.

Relevant to what Jim had said earlier about the masses going along with what the power elite wanted for the sake of their jobs or whatever, I reminded him that I had earlier referred to W. J. Ghent's *Our Benevolent Feudalism* written in 1902. And in "The Next Step: A Benevolent Feudalism" (*The Independent*, April 3, 1902), Ghent wrote that the

> ... coming status ... will be something in the nature of a Benevolent Feudalism. ... Group fidelity ... is already observable. ... The autocrats ... will distribute benefits to the degree that makes a tolerant, if not satisfied people. ... A person of offensive activity may be denied work in every feudal shop and on every feudal farm from one end of the country to the other. ... His actions will be promptly communicated to the banded autocracy of dukes, earls and marquises of industries. ... The individual security of place and livelihood of its members will then depend on the harmony of their utterances and acts with the wishes of the great nobles; and so long as they rightly fulfill their functions their recompense will be generous.
>
> They will be at once the assuagers of popular suspicion and discontent and the providers of moral and intellectual anodynes for the barons. ... A host of economists, preachers and editors will be ready to show indisputably that the evolution taking place is for the best interests of all. ... What the barons will most dread will be the collective assertion of the villains at the polls; but this, from experience, they will know to be a thing of no immediate danger. By the putting forward of

a hundred irrelevant issues they can hopelessly divide the voters at each election; or, that failing, there is always to be trusted as a last resort the cry of impending panic. ... Two divisions of the courtier class are the judges and the politicians. ... They must satisfy the demands of the multitude, and yet, on the other hand, they must obey the commands from above. ... The nobles will have attained to complete power, and the motive and operation of Government will have become simply the registering and administering of their collective will. ... Armed forces will, of course, be employed to overawe the discontented and to quiet unnecessary turbulence. Unlike the armed forces of the old feudalism, the nominal control will be that of the State. ... When the new order is in full swing, so comprehensive and so exact will be the social and political control that it will be exercised in a constantly widening scope. ... Peace [and stability] will be the main desideratum. ... A happy blending of generosity and firmness will characterize all dealings with open discontent. ... [To] the prevention of discontent ... the teachings of the schools and colleges, the sermons, the editorials ... and even the plays at the theaters will be skillfully and persuasively molded.

Jim's reaction to this quote was one of amazement as to how it already so accurately described conditions in the United States (and the world) today.

I lamented that Jim was probably, unfortunately, accurate in his gloomy assessment about the world ending with a "whimper," and I told him that founding father Samuel Adams had said, "While the people are virtuous they cannot be subdued, but when once they lose their virtue they will be ready to surrender their liberties to the first external or internal invader." I then asked Jim if he was familiar with Alexis DeTocqueville's famous quote: "Not until I went into the churches of America and heard her pulpits flame with righteousness did I understand the secret of their genius and power. America is great because America is good, and if America ever ceases to be good, America will cease to be great."

Jim acknowledged that he was familiar with that quote, so I told him that additionally in DeTocqueville's *Democracy in America* (1840), the French author and statesman expressed concerns regarding potential despotisms as follows:

> Above this race of men stands an immense and tutelary power, which takes upon itself alone to secure their gratifications and to watch over their fate. ... After having thus successively taken each member of the community in its powerful grasp and fashioned him at will, the supreme power then extends its arm over the whole community. ... The will of man is not shattered, but softened, bent, and guided. ... It does not tyrannize, but it compresses, enervates, extinguishes, and stupefies a people, till each nation is reduced to nothing better than a flock of timid and industrious animals, of which the government is the shepherd.

Jim quickly remarked that DeTocqueville seemed to be talking about the world socialist government desired by the power elite. And I told him that I thought he was exactly right, and that in my opinion, the only hope for Americans to avoid such an undesirable future was to return to being "good" (e.g., stop the slaughter of innocent preborn children by abortion, gruesome fetal experiments, etc.) by once again following biblical moral principles upon which this nation was founded.

Jim was in complete agreement, but asserted that it would not be easy given the hold that secular humanism had upon the country. I agreed and recounted how *Humanist Manifesto* signer Charles Francis Potter in 1930 authored *Humanism: A New Religion,* in which he proclaimed: "Education is thus a most powerful ally of humanism. What can the theistic Sunday schools, meeting for an hour once a week, and teaching only a fraction of the children, do to stem the tide of a five-day program of humanistic teaching?"

I stressed that the public schools had been the primary vehicle by which secular humanism had been promoted in the United States after Bible-reading and vocal prayer had been eliminated from public schools by the U.S. Supreme Court in the early 1960s. I further explained that in 1976, Paul Blanshard, a leading secular humanist, in an article had noted that the fact that "Johnny is in school until he is sixteen tends to lead toward the elimination of religious superstition." And another leading secular humanist, Sidney Hook, in a publication a year later remarked that religious beliefs would be undermined "only by indirection, [by which] I mean the development of a critical attitude in all our educational institutions that will aim to make students less credulous to claims that transcend their reflective experience." Then a few years later, in a prize-winning essay in *The Humanist* in 1983, John Dunphy wrote: "The battle for humankind's future must be waged and won in the public school classroom ... between the rotting corpse of Christianity ... and the new faith of humanism. ... Humanism will emerge triumphant."

Jim dejectedly replied that it seemed that secular humanism had indeed been triumphant, and I supported his conclusion by pointing out that not too long ago the Josephson Institute of Ethics polled more that twenty thousand middle and high school students and found that an amazing forty-seven percent acknowledged that they had stolen something from a store in the past twelve months! Jim asked if our public school teachers and secular humanists actually tell students to steal, and I indicated that they do not do that. However, they do say the student is an autonomous moral decision-maker who should make up her or his own mind about what is right or wrong based upon the situation (situation ethics). I asked Jim to think about the profound moral implications of having students adopt that attitude toward life.

Not only has secular humanism been triumphant in the United States, but also in the whole world. For example, on October 28, 2014, the national news media reported that Pope Francis was open to evolution (a basic tenet of secular humanism) and had said that "God is not a magician with a magic wand." In other words, God did not simply "create" Adam and Eve as *The Holy Bible* states. Does the pope therefore believe that the miracle of Jesus and the loaves and fishes is also not true? Think of the tremendous implications of this lack of faith as well !

Jim said, "Look, you have made some very interesting points with quotes by Cecil Rhodes, Woodrow Wilson, FDR and others, but how do you know these aren't independent actions? How do you know they are all part of the same plot or scheme?"

I replied, "The answer lies in Theodore Marburg!"

"Who?" Jim asked.

"That's right," I stated, "and most people have never heard of Marburg." I explained that Marburg became friends with Woodrow Wilson (who would be a progressive) when they were students at Johns Hopkins University in the 1880s. This is also when the Fabian Society was formed and where Wilhelm Wundt (grandfather member of the Illuminati in the late 1700s and code named Raphael) first American Ph.D., G. Stanley Hall, mentored John Dewey (who would become the "Father of Progressive Education," and a signer of the first *Humanist Manifesto* in 1993.

"Jim," I said, "I am going to read to you something extensive, but it will show how Marburg is the key to putting Wilson, the progressives, humanism, Cecil Rhodes, international financiers, and others together in a world government secret plan." I then began to read from Jennings Wise's *Woodrow Wilson: Disciple of Revolution* (1938):

> Marburg has no counterpart in history. At times, even
> Machiavelli seems, compared to him, like a novice at the game

of politics. ... Wilson, also under the Johns Hopkins influence, had now come to believe in the necessity of an Anglo-American alliance. ... Marburg decided to take a special course in economics and political science at Oxford. There he proposed to acquaint himself with the Fabians. ... In England, he soon met ... William T. Stead [one of Cecil Rhodes' top three members of his secret Society of the Elect to "take the government of the whole world," in Rhodes' words] of the *Pall Mall Gazette* [and] Bernard Shaw. ... Marburg thought peace in Europe could only be re-established and maintained by a league of nations to enforce peace. The question was, therefore, how could Marburg and Stead do this? ... Now it was that Marburg saw the light. ... What then if Carnegie and his unlimited wealth, the international financiers, and the socialists could be organized in a movement to compel the formation of a league to enforce peace? ... In short, Marburg concluded that the liberalization of the government of the world through the medium of a league of nations, with power residing in the hands of the international financiers to control its councils and enforce peace, would prove a specific [remedy] for all the political ills of mankind!

This plan was one which could not be concretely expressed, since it required a certain amount of secrecy in its execution. ... It was imperative that its financial aspects be screened, that the money interests behind it be held under cover, that the whole movement be cloaked with the guise of pure humanism. ... In short, the scheme must be whispered only to those ... who could recognize the need of appearing to be working only for universal peace, while educating the world up to an internationalism that would demand political sacrifices on the part of the nations. ... Stead outlined to the world, in a remarkable article first published in *The Nation*, Marburg's scheme of a league of nations to enforce peace.

Only through a world court backed by an international

police, could justice be done, he declared. ... Marburg was at Heidelberg [1900–1901] where ... he had gone to study German Socialism and Social Democracy. Returning to his old plan of studying politics in Germany, Wilson was on the point of applying for a year's leave of absence from Princeton to go to Heidelberg too. ... [But] in 1902, ... Woodrow Wilson was elected President of Princeton University! In 1906, Marburg hurried home to found the. ... American Association for International Conciliation, with himself as President, and with ... Carnegie, Nicholas Murray Butler, ... Paul Warburg, Otto Kahn, Bernard Baruch, ... and international bankers on its council. It was then that this indefatigable man published his *Toward an Enduring Peace* in which he virtually outlined to the world what was expected of the Powers. ... Marburg knew that what politicians feared most are organized votes.

Therefore he decided to complete the organization of the American Branch of the League to Enforce Peace. Ostensibly an agency to promote a league of nations, it was also to enforce suitable action on Wilson and the Democratic Party.

Following the long quote I read to Jim about Marburg, I explained that there were those who seemed privy to the power elite's plan for Woodrow Wilson. In Stephen Wise's 1910 autobiography, *Challenging Years,* Wise wrote:

On a Sunday before his election as Governor of New Jersey, in 1910, I made a nonpolitical address before the Trenton YMCA. To these fellow Jerseymen, of Woodrow Wilson I said, "On Tuesday the president of Princeton University will be elected governor of your state. He will not complete his term of office as governor. In November, 1912, he will be elected President of the United States. In March, 1917, he will be inaugurated for the second time as President."

That Woodrow Wilson was under the control of the PE can be seen from the following quote by Curtis Dall in his book, *Fdr: My Exploited Father-In-Law:*

> ... Occasionally, on a Saturday morning in the summer of 1912, Bernard Baruch would walk into the Democratic Headquarters with Woodrow Wilson in tow, "leading him like one would a poodle on a string" Wilson would be quite solemn-faced in appearance. ... According to my friend Wilson would be given his special "indoctrination course" in politics, by several of the top advisers assembled there. The course consisted chiefly of outlining to him and his agreeing in principle to: Aiding and pushing the projected Federal Reserve Bank Legislation through Congress when Paul Warburg approved the final draft of the opposed Act, then being worked on. ... [And] if called upon, to lend a sympathetic ear and aid indicated "policy" if war should break out in Europe. ... Wilson dutifully received and absorbed his indoctrination, shook hands all around, and then departed. ...

At this point, Jim related to me that he was becoming convinced that what I had been telling him was correct, but he then asked if I had any persuasive quotes by power elite members in this twenty-first century to bolster my argument. I proceeded to read to him from David Rockefeller's *Memoirs* (2002), in which one finds the following:

> Some even believe we [the Rockefellers] are part of a secret cabal working against the best interests of the United States, characterizing my family and me as "internationalists" and of conspiring with others around the world to build a more integrated global political and economic structure—one world, if you will. If that's the charge, I stand guilty, and I am proud of it.

Jim was amazed that David Rockefeller admitted he was part of a "secret cabal" for "one world," and he wondered why the press/media had not picked up on this. I told Jim that David Brooks in *The New York Times* had written a long book review about Rockefeller's book, but nowhere in it did he mention the "secret cabal" quote. I went on to say that I tried to get a *USA Today* reporter who had written about the Bushes and Skull & Bones to write about what Rockefeller had said, but he declined.

I explained to Jim that we have not really had an independent press for a long time, and I quoted John Swinton (editorial page editor of *The New York Times*, 1860–1870) as saying to a gathering of journalists at the Twilight Club in New York City on April 12, 1883:

> There is no such thing in America as an independent press, unless it is in the country towns. You know it and I know it. There is not one of you who dare to write his honest opinions, and if you did you know beforehand they would never appear in print. ... The business of the New York journalist is to destroy the truth, to lie outright, to pervert, to vililfy, to fawn at the feet of Mammon. ... You know this and I know it, and what folly is this to be toasting an "independent press." We are the tools and vassals of rich men behind the scenes. We are the jumping-jacks; they pull the strings and we dance. Our talents, our possibilities and our lives are all the property of other men. We are intellectual prostitutes.

Following this, I gave Jim four examples from the twentieth century to back up my point. On February 9, 1917, U.S. Rep. Oscar Calloway inserted the following statement in the *Congressional Record:*

> In March 1915 the J. P. Morgan interests, the steel, shipbuilding, and powder interests, and their subsidiary organizations

got together twelve men high up in the newspaper world and employed them to select the most influential newspapers in the United States and sufficient number of them to control generally the policy of the daily press of the United States. These twelve men worked the problem out by selecting 179 newspapers, and then began, by an elimination process, to retain only those necessary for the purpose of controlling the general policy of the daily press throughout the country. They found it was only necessary to purchase the control of twenty-five of the greatest newspapers. The twenty-five papers were agreed upon; emissaries were sent to purchase the policy, national and international, of these papers; an agreement was reached; the policy of the papers was bought, to be paid for by the month; an editor was furnished for each paper to properly supervise and edit information. ...

J. P. Morgan was the banker in the United States who was helping to facilitate Cecil Rhodes' secret Society of the Elect's plan to "take the government of the whole world." And Rhodes wanted to control four main aspects of life—politics, economics, education, and journalism. Therefore, Morgan's takeover of the press in this country was toward the fulfillment of Rhodes' plan.

The second example was from Christopher Hobhouse's *Oxford As It Was and Is Today* (1939), in which he revealed:

It is the Editor of *The* [London] *Times* and his circle of associates ... [who] elect to consider themselves the powers behind the scenes. The duty of purveying honest news is elevated in their eyes into the prerogative of dictating opinion. It is at All Souls [College, Oxford University] that they meet to decide just how little they will let their readers know.

The third example is from Herman Dinsmore (foreign editor of *The New York Times* from 1951 to 1960), who wrote in *All The*

*News That Fits* (1969) that "*The New York Times* today is deliberately pitched to the so-called liberal point of view. ... Positively and negatively, the weight of *The Times* has generally fallen on the side of the communists since the end of World War II." Four years after Dinsmore's book was published, power elite member David Rockefeller in the August 10, 1973 *New York Times* wrote a glowing op-ed article praising the communist dictator Chairman Mao, even after most people knew he had killed millions of his own innocent people.

Rockefeller was chairman of the Council on Foreign Relations (CFR) from 1970 to 1985 and chairman emeritus since then. And, as example number four, in the October 30, 1993 edition of *The Washington Post,* that newspaper's ombudsman, Richard Harwood, described the role of the CFR's press and media members in the following manner: "Their membership is an acknowledgment of their ascension into the American ruling class [where] they do not merely analyze and interpret foreign policy for the United States; they help make it."

Rockefeller once told Congressman William Dannemeyer that some men are born to rule, but most men are born to be ruled. Power elite member Rockefeller was and is helping to facilitate fellow power elite member Cecil Rhodes' plan for world control, including the use of journalism via the journalists' CFR membership.

As an example of how the press/media are controlled today, I told Jim to look at the case of Egypt. I said, "Jim, do you remember just a few years ago when the press/media were constantly publicizing the protests against the authoritarian Hosni Mubarak in Egypt and calling for democratic reform? Well, Jim, where is that press/media now when the authoritarian Gen. Abdel Fattah Saeed Hussein Khalil el-Sisi took over Egypt in a military coup?"

Jim responded, "Yeah, you are right! Where are they?"

I said, "Their controllers, the PE, through carefully selected editors, have assigned them to cover other news instead."

I then asked Jim if he didn't think it strange that the press wasn't curious about cargo planes with opium going from Afghanistan to Shiite Iran before going to Sunni Turkey when supposedly the Shiites and Sunnis are bitter enemies. According to Paul Williams, author of *Crescent Moon Rising* (2013), the CIA has for years known about these cargo flights, and a major beneficiary of this has been Fethullah Gulen who is living in Pennsylvania and has established many charter schools in the U.S., Turkey, and the Caspian area  According to Williams, there's a CIA agent in every one of these Caspian schools. And for some reason, the press hasn't seen fit to investigate all of this! Could it be because the PE doesn't want them to look into it?

Jim was impressed with my information concerning the press/media's control by the PE, and he requested the same type of evidence concerning the other three areas (politics, economics, and education) Cecil Rhodes desired to control. I explained to him that the Rhodes network worked with a number of other groups like Skull & Bones (S&B), and that in the late 1800s S&B member William Whitney (and his son) developed a strategy to contribute heavily to both major political parties and alternate power so that the public believed they had choice in voting when they really did not. This is why for many decades (about sixty-five years), neither the Democrat nor Republican parties has occupied the presidency for two back-to-back eight-year terms. George H. W. Bush (whom David Rockefeller said was "one of us") was not re-elected in 1992 after succeeding Ronald Reagan in 1988.

Jim then commented, "I understand all that, but most of what you have told me involves the past. For your theory to work, you have to demonstrate predictability. In other words, have you—based upon your theory of PE control and manipulation—been able to predict events?" Jim had raised a legitimate point, and so told him that while many pundits had said President Obama would not be re-elected in 2012, I said that according to the PE plan, he would be re-elected, and I was proven correct. I next told him that according to the planned alternation of power, the next president elected in November 2016 would be a Republican (probably Jeb Bush), who would be narrowly re-elected in 2020 (probably due to an "October surprise"), and that person would be followed by a Democrat in November 2024 (probably a woman) because Alice Bailey in 1933 said the World Federation of Nations would be "taking rapid shape" in 2025.

Regarding predictability in economics, I told Jim that in the January 9, 1988, edition of *The Economist,* they predicted that a world currency called the Phoenix would appear in 2018. Supporting this, I told Jim to look at the October 6, 2009, edition of *The Independent* in which Robert Fisk wrote "The Demise of the Dollar," and referred to

> secret meetings [that] have already been held by finance ministers and central bank governors in Russia, China, Japan and Brazil to work on the scheme [to have a basket of currencies for oil], which will mean that oil will no longer be priced in dollars. ... Chinese financial sources believe President Barack Obama is too busy fixing the U.S. economy to concentrate on the extraordinary implications of the transition from the dollar in nine years' time. The current deadline for the currency transition is 2018.

Similarly the next year, on September 1, 2010, Dr. Alessandro Sassoli was interviewed by *Coin Update* regarding his idea beginning in 1996 for a new global currency, a project of the United Future World Currency (UFWO) organization. And in this interview, he stated: "The world is evolving very fast. Maybe in just eight years time, it might be possible to introduce a new super-national currency like the UFWC by 2018."

I continued to talk to Jim about predictability and economics by citing the more recent *Wall Street Journal* article for January 28, 2015, titled, "Currency Tumult Stokes Big Bets." I told him that the article began by stating: "A surging dollar is pummeling currencies around the globe amid efforts to boost economic growth, prompting a wave of investor bets to profit from the upheaval. Many global central banks are weakening their currencies as they try to counter signs of economic gloom. ... "

I also referred Jim to *Moneynews* (February 11, 2015) titled, "El-Erian: Currency War 'Can Persist for a While'," in which Mohamed El-Erian, chief economic advisor at Allianz, wrote about "financial markets' willingness to assume and maintain risk postures that are not validated by the economy's fundamentals. With central banks pushing for increasingly large financial risk-taking, this is no easy feat." I told Jim that the PE controls the Bank for International Settlements (BIS), which is the world's central bank for all of the nations' central banks. Continuing with the *Moneynews* article, I explained that in it, David Woo, head of global currency research at Bank of America Merrill Lynch, indicted that he, too, is concerned about the currency war, saying "at this point, FX volatility has become the prime driver in global volatility [according to CNBC]. If everyone is playing this game, you have no choice but to play it, because otherwise you get left behind. ... "

Relevant to my prediction of a world currency by 2018, I explained to Jim that the PE could use these signs of "economic gloom" by offering a world currency to eliminate the uncertainties of currency volatility.

Jim accepted my analysis, but then said the fulfillment of my predictions was of a general nature, and he asked if my theory applied, for example, to specific predictions of terrorist activity. I told him that I had made such predictions which came to pass. I told Jim that in the October 1, 2003, *Centre Daily Times (Pennsylvania)*, I indicated that terrorists might "try to ... disrupt our supply of electricity." And on April 16, 2013, a terrorist attack occurred at about one a.m. when they cut the fiber cable around the Metcalf power substation southeast of San Jose, California, cut off some local 911 services, and fired one hundred rounds from a high-powered rifle at several electrical transformers (the perpetrators have not yet been caught).

Secondly, in my NewsWithViews (NWV) column for April 15, 2013, I wrote that Iranian-sponsored terrorists could attack locations in the United States with incendiary devices, and on that same afternoon two locations in Boston were attacked by two Muslim terrorist brothers using explosive devices. Thirdly, in the same NWV column, I referred to terrorists derailing trains, and a week later (April 22), Canadian police had announced they had just thwarted terrorists' plan to derail passenger trains in the greater Toronto area (Canada is part of NATO, which these terrorists would probably say had killed innocent Muslim civilians in bombing raids overseas). Canadian authorities said the terror suspects had received support from Al Qaeda elements in Iran).

Fourthly, in the same NWV column, I said terrorists could use contaminants (I meant lethal ones), and the next day (April 16) an envelope containing the highly toxic ricin was received at the U.S. Capitol for U.S. Senator Roger Wicker from Mississippi. A similar envelope was received the following day for President Obama at the White House.

Fifthly, in the same NWV column, I mentioned that terrorists could hack into our banking system and wipe out or withdraw money from people's accounts. And eight days later (April 23), the Syrian Electronic Army (pro-Assad hackers) hacked into the Associated Press website and posted a bogus news item about the White House being attacked and President Obama injured. This, in turn, caused the stock market to drop, resulting in some people losing a lot of money.

Sixthly, in My April 15, 2013, NWV column, I predicted that terrorists could set an apartment complex in this country on fire at night, and on May 27, 2015, the *Los Angeles Times* reported that the L.A. Police Department's anti-terrorism division arrested Dawud Abdulwali "on suspicion of arson in connection with a fire that destroyed a downtown Los Angeles apartment complex" on December 8, 2014, at 1:20 a.m. (night). Abdulwali may have been a "lone wolf," but he may also have been prompted by ISIS, which was looking at how long it took for him to be found and arrested. The time between the fire and his arrest was about 170 days. Suppose ISIS now calculated one of its members here could have as many as 170 days to set as many apartment (or forest) fires as possible!

Lastly, at the end of my February 17, 2014, NWV column, I posed the threat of terrorists using toothpaste tube bombs and said they could use cold cream jars. Three days later, Diane Sawyer on ABC's "World News Tonight" mentioned they had received a report that terrorists might use cosmetics such as cold cream!

I then told Jim that in the future, he should watch for terrorists in Europe and the United States setting fires in forests, as well as setting off IEDs (improvised explosive devices) at important places (e.g., on or under interstate highway bridges as fuel tankers pass by).

Jim was extremely impressed with these examples, and asked what the PE was up to now. I said, "Just look around you at what is happening. The PE uses crises to gain more and more control. President Obama has let many illegal immigrants (including children) into this country even though they had many illnesses, even contagious ones. Now there is a spreading outbreak of measles, with calls for mandatory vaccinations and no exceptions based upon religious grounds.

"In addition, there has just been a news announcement that perhaps 80 million Americans' Social Security numbers, etc. have been compromised by hackers gaining access to the health insurance giant Anthem's computer records. The solution, of course, will be more and more government controls, perhaps requiring each computer having a unique identifying number belonging to a single person, who would also be identified by that number, which would be required to make phone calls, make credit card purchases. etc.—again, more and more control over our lives exercised by the PE."

Jim was finally becoming convinced about the validity of what I was saying, and then asked about the other area that Cecil Rhodes wanted especially to control—education. I said, "Jim, for the answer to that question, I suggest you look at the final chapter in this book. It is about the current controversu surrounding the latest educational reform movement, Common Core, and its background."

# Chapter 11

# Common Core

There is a great controversy today over the educational reform movement known as Common Core (CC). Many people have offered specific criticisms of the movement, but they generally look at CC in isolation. However, it is important to understand the background of CC, and a good starting point for that begins with the Illuminati, which began on May 1, 1776.

The fundamental purpose of the Illuminati was to do away with existing authority (e.g., monarchical, religious, etc.) and adopt the principle of its founder, Adam Weishaupt, which was that they, the Illuminati or Enlightened, knew what was best for people. The leaders of CC today also believe they know, even better than parents, what is best in education for children in the United States. Relevant to education, certain members of the Illuminati became tutors to princes, who would then become czars, kings, etc. (e.g., Alexander I of Russia) and be under the influence of the Illuminati.

In terms of what we know today as elementary and secondary education, Illuminati member Johann Heinrich Pestalozzi (a Swiss, code-named Alfred) had the greatest influence. According to Will Monroe's *History of the Pestalozzian Method in the United States* (1907), the educational ideas of Pestalozzi began to be printed in journals and textbooks in the United States in 1806. They began to be used in some school systems, especially in New England where they were viewed favorably be the intelligentsia of Horace Mann's day. This was the first half of the 1800s, and Mann became known as the "Father of the American Public Education."

Utopian socialist Robert Owen visited Pestalozzi at Yverdon, Switzerland, in 1818, and applied the Illuminist's educational principles in Britain and America. In 1825, Owen established the first commune in the United States in New Harmony, Indiana. Joining Owen in 1828 was Frances Wright (formerly Madame Francoise D'Arusmont from France) who, with Owen's son Robert Dale Owen and Orestes Brownson, formed the Workingmen's Party in New York.

According to *A Concise History of the American Republic* (vol. 1) by Samuel Morison, Henry Steele Commager, and William Leuchtenburg, Frances Wright became "a lecture-platform apostle of … a system which she called 'National, Rational, Republican Education, Free for All, at the Expense of All, Conducted under the Guardianship of the State,' apart from the contaminating influence of parents." After Brownson became a Christian, he revealed in *The Works Of Orestes Brownson* (twenty volumes) that their plan in establishing their political party was as follows:

> The great object was to get rid of Christianity, and to convert our churches into halls of science. The plan was not to make open attacks upon religion, although we might belabor the clergy and bring them into contempt where we could; but to establish a system of state—we said national—schools, from which all religion was to be excluded, in which nothing was to be taught except such knowledge as is verifiable by the senses, and to which all parents were to be compelled by law to send their children. Our complete plan was to take the children from their parents at the age of twelve or eighteen months, and to have them nursed, fed, clothed, and trained in these schools at the public expense; but

at any rate, we were to have godless schools for all the children of the country. ... The plan has been successfully pursued, ... and the whole action of the country on the subject has taken the direction we sought to give it. One of the principal movers of the scheme had no mean share in organizing the Smithsonian Institute.

Brownson further revealed that the connection between the Workingmen's Party, Robert Owen (father of Robert Dale Owen), Pestalozzi, and Horace Mann is very important. In *Horace Mann: Educational Statesman,* Heidelberg College (Ohio) professor E. I. F. Williams wrote:

The "workingmen's movement" was an organization of the liberals in opposition to the conservative order. ... Its members were the radical wing of the Jacksonian democracy. In 1831 a large convention [of the Workingmen's Party] made up of farmers and workmen was held in Boston. ... Leaders such as Horace Mann [in Massachusetts] ... urged their cause. Education was advanced as the surest and best method of advancing their aspirations. ... Labor leaders were enthusiastic about education in tax-supported schools. ... Education soon took first place among the reforms they demanded. They urged the necessity of an "equal, universal, republican system of education." ... Reform was the watch-word of the day. ... More than two hundred communists utopias were established. ... For two or three decades, they centered the attention of the country on socialistic and communistic schemes for human betterment. One of the most famous of the communities was established at New Harmony, Indiana, by Robert Owen.

In *Horace Mann : Educat0nal Statesman,* E. I. F. Williams related that Robert Owen brought William McClure, "father of American geology," to organize his school. He first introduced the Pestalozzian system into the United States. ... Later, the Pestalozzian movement spread to other sections [of the country], and among its enthusiastic champions were Horace Mann. ... Very soon [after New Harmony] another society based on Owen's principles was begun at Yellow Springs, Ohio, where Antioch College was to be founded.

Horace Mann was president of Antioch College from 1853 until his death on August 2, 1859. In 1837, Mann had established the first "normal" (public) school in the United States as part of his effort to promote nonsectarian education.

In 1848, the *Communist Manifesto* was published, including Plank No. 10, which provided for a "combination of education with industrial production" (a type of school-to-work approach). Nine years later in 1857, the National Education Association (NEA, until 1870 called the National Teachers Association) was founded and emphasized the importance of teachers in children's education. Following this, California State Superintendent of Public Instruction John Swett in 1864 declared: "The vulgar impression that parents have a legal right to dictate to teachers is entirely erroneous. ... "

In 1879, Illuminati member Kirchenrat Karl Kasimir Wundt's (code name Raphael) grandson, Wilhelm Wundt established the first laboratory in experimental psychology at the University of Leipzig (Pavlov studied there in 1884). The first of his American students was G. Stanley Hall, who would become John Dewey's mentor at Johns Hopkins University (where Dewey received his doctorate in 1884). Educational experimentalists James McKeen Cattell, Charles Judd, and James Earl Russell also received doctorates from Wundt. Dewey later become known as the "Father of Progressive Education," even though Dewey himself used that appellation in reference to Francis Parker, who had studied the ideas of Pestalozzi when in Europe.

Twelve years after receiving his doctorate, Dewey established in January 1896 his own laboratory school at the University of Chicago, an institution of higher learning well-endowed by John D. Rockefeller, Sr. This oil magnate in 1902 chartered the General Education Board, and appointed Frederick Gates (a Baptist minister) as chairman. Gates wrote Occasional Letter, No. 1 (published in *The World's Work* in 1912) in which he remarked: "In our dream, we have limitless resources, and the people yield themselves with perfect docility to our molding hand. The present educational conventions fade from our minds; and, unhampered by tradition, we work our own good will upon a grateful and responsive rural folk."

On October 12, 1917, *The New York Times* published Judge John Hylan's comments about a letter by Dr. Abraham Flexner (secretary of the General Education Board and formerly of the Carnegie Foundation describing a "secret conference" of New York City Board of Education's members to elect a board president who would institute a type of school-to-work outcome-based education program. Five years later, *The New York Times* (March 27, 1922) covered a speech by Judge Hylan after he had become mayor of New York City. In the speech, Mayor Hylan said:

> The warning of Theodore Roosevelt has much timeliness today, for the real menace of our republic is this invisible government which like a giant octopus sprawls its slimy length over city, State and nation. ... The little coterie of powerful international bankers virtually run the United States Government for their own selfish purposes. ... These international bankers and Rockefeller-Standard Oil interests control the majority of newspapers and magazines in this country.

Mayor Hylan quoted from Frederick Gates' paper mentioned

above, and then said, "This is the kind of education the coolies receive in China, but we are not going to stand for it in these United States. One of my first acts as Mayor was to pitch out, bag and baggage, from the educational system of our city the Rockefeller agents and the Gary plan of education to fit the children for the mill and factory."

Following the theme of the Illuminati and Common Core proponents that "they know what is best for the rest of us," Arthur Calhoun in 1919 authored the third volume in his series, *A Social History of the American Family*, which became a widely used social service textbook. In it, he noted that "the child passes more and more into the custody of community experts," and he also elaborated that

> the new view is that the higher and more obligatory relation is to society rather than to the family; the family goes back to the age of savagery while the state belongs to the age of civilization. The modern individual is a world citizen [a view of the Illuminati], served by the world, and home interests can no longer be supreme. ... As soon as the new family, consisting of only the parents and the children, stood forth, society saw how many were unfit for parenthood and began to realize the need for community care. ... As familism weakens, society has to assume a larger parenthood.
>
> The school begins to assume responsibility for the functions thrust upon it. ... The kindergarten grows downward toward the cradle and there arises talk of neighborhood nurseries. ... It seems clear that at least in its early stages, socialism will mean an increased amount of social control. ... We may expect in the socialist commonwealth a system of public educational agencies that will begin with the nursery and follow the individual through life. ... Those persons that experience alarm at the thought of intrinsic changes in family institutions should

remember that in the light of social evolution, nothing is right or valuable in itself.

Remember the above references to "cradle" and "follow the individual through life" when reading a later part of this chapter describing a letter written by National Center on Education and the Economy president Marc Tucker on November 11, 1992, to Hillary Clinton about Bill Clinton's presidential victory giving them a chance to implement their "cradle to grave" plan for everyone.

In the 1920s, "Father of Progressive Education" (and later National Education Association honorary president) John Dewey went to the Soviet Union and authored an article in the December 5, 1928, edition of *The New Republic,* in which he described

the marvelous development of progressive educational ideas and practices under the fostering care of the Bolshevist government ... the required collective and cooperative mentality. ... The great task of the school is to counteract and transform those domestic and neighborhood tendencies ... the influence of home and Church. ... In order to accomplish this end, the teachers must in the first place know with great detail and accuracy just what the conditions are to which pupils are subject in the home [remember this when reading about Common Core's collection of large amounts of personal data]. ... One of the most interesting pedagogical innovations ... to discover the actual conditions that influence pupils in their out-of-school life ... [is using] the themes of written work, the compositions of pupils, and also a detailed study throughout the year of home and family budgets. ... The institution of the family is being sapped indirectly rather than by frontal attack. ... There is no word one hears oftener than Gruppe, and all sorts of groups are instituted that militate against the primary social importance of the family unit.

In consequence, to anyone who looks at the matter cold-bloodedly, free from sentimental associations clustering about the historic family institution, a most interesting sociological experimentation is taking place. ... Our special concern here is with the role of the schools in building up forces and factors whose natural effect is to undermine the importance and uniqueness of family life. ... The earliest section of the school system, dealing with children from three to seven, aims to keep children under its charge six, eight, and ten hours a day, and in ultimate ideal this procedure is to be universal and compulsory. ... Reference to this phase of Soviet education may perhaps be suitably concluded by a quotation from Lenin: 'We must declare openly what is concealed, namely, the political function of the school. ... It is to construct communist society.'

The next year (1929), Edward Thorndike (trained by Wundtians in the United States) and Arthur Gates authored *Elementary Principles of Education,* in which one reads:

Traditionally the elementary school has been primarily devoted to teaching the fundamental subjects, the three R's, and closely related disciplines. ... Artificial exercises, like drills on phonetics, multiplication tables, and formal writing movements, are used to a wasteful degree. Subjects such as arithmetic, language, and history include content that is intrinsically of little value. ...

(In a later part of this chapter, NEA president Catherine Barrett will make a similar comment in 1973.) Pursuing these "progressive education" attitudes, Thorndike will produce new spellers, math texts, dictionaries, and textbooks on education and educational testing.

A year later (1930), the "Dick and Jane" basal reading series begins, using the "look-say" or "whole word" method of reading instruction Up until this time, there was a high rate of literacy among the people of the United States, but the consequences of "progressive educators" using the "look-say" approach (instead of the highly successful intensive phonics method) will prove disastrous, causing a growing problem of illiteracy.

Four years after the look-say "Dick and Jane" basal reading series was introduced, in 1934 *Conclusions and Recommendations* (the last of a seventeen-volume study concerning American education) of the Commission on Social Studies of the American Historical association was published. The work of the commission was financed ($340,000) by the Carnegie Corporation. Commenting on the document in *The New Republic* article "A New Education for A New America" (July 29, 1936), British socialist Prof. Harold Laski remarked that the volume contained "a content of teaching which frankly admits that the age of government control has arrived. … For, at bottom, and stripped of its carefully neutral phrases, the report is an educational program for a socialist America."

Two years after Laski wrote this, on March 1, 1938, according to George Mosse's *Nazi Culture* in the chapter "The Key: Education of Youth," under the Nazis (National socialists),

> the textbooks were increasingly National socialist, the teachers were regimented. … The individual states were abolished. … The Nazis attempted to unify the school system, as they "meshed the gears" of all other activities in the Third Reich. … Changes in the curriculum brought all schools closer together. … Social pressures aided the Nazis in getting rid of the influence of the older generation. …

Under Common Core, assessments drive curricula to unify nationally education in America, and school systems' teachers become to a certain extent regimented in preparing students for the assessments (getting correct answers is not enough, but also knowing how), whether in individual classrooms or for the college boards.

"Getting rid of the influence of the older generation" in the United States was also important for the power elite. And the way to do this was through "critical thinking." Three years after the Nazis began the educational program mentioned above, Edward Glaser authored *An Experiment in the Development of Critical Thinking* (1941). It was one the first books on the subject and followed the psychodrama and sociometry work of Rumanian psychiatrist Jacob Moreno in the early part of the twentieth century.

Critical thinking developed into critiquing, which in turn developed into criticizing the values of "the older generation." The purpose was to establish a "generation gap," with the new generation adopting more humanistic than biblical values.

By the end of World War II, the National Education Association (NEA) was promoting world government. In the *NEA Journal* (January 1946), Joy Elmer Morgan (editor of the *NEA Journal,* 1921–1955) wrote "The Teacher and World Government," in which he proclaimed:

> In the struggle to establish an adequate world government, the teacher ... can do much to prepare the hearts and minds of children for global understanding and cooperation. ... At the very top of all the agencies which will assure the coming of world government must stand the school, the teacher, and the organized profession.

Similarly two years later, Sir Julian Huxley (first director-general of UNESCO) authored *UNESCO: Its Purpose and Its Philosophy* (1948), in which he wrote of UNESCO's educational program that it could "stress the ultimate need for world political unity and familiarize all peoples with the implications of the transfer of full sovereignty from separate nations to a world organization ... political unification in some sort of world government will be required. ... "

Of course, if there were to be a world government, something would have to be done to bring capitalist and communist governments together. In 1953 Ford Foundation president H. Rowan Gaither told Norman Dodd (research director for the congressional Reece Committee) that the foundation was operating under directives from the White House "to the effect that we should make every effort to so alter life in the United States as to make possible a comfortable merger with the Soviet Union."

As mentioned earlier, "Father of Progressive Education" John Dewey very much admired what the Soviets (remember that the second S in U.S.S.R. stands for "socialist") were doing. He taught at Columbia University from 1905 to 1930, and by the early 1950s, the Deweyites had taken control of Columbia's Teachers College. In *A History of Teachers College: Columbia University* (1954), Lawrence Cremin *et al.* explained that

> the single most powerful education force in the world is at twentieth Street and Broadway in New York City. Your children's teachers go there for advanced training. ... With one hundred thousand alumni, TC has managed to seat about one-third of the presidents and deans now [1953] in office at accredited U.S. teaching training schools. Its graduates make up about twenty percent of all our public school teachers. Over a fourth of the superintendents of schools in the one-hundred sixty-eight U.S. cities with at least fifty thousand population are TC-trained.

Relevant to the effort to move us toward a "comfortable merger" with the Soviet Union as mentioned above, in 1960 HEW published *Soviet Education Programs*, wherein one reads: "... wherever we went, we felt the pulse of the Soviet government's desire to educate and train a new generation of technically skilled citizens. ... U.S.S.R. plans to bring all secondary school children into labor education and training experiences through the regular school program."

Beginning in the early 1960s, the Deweyites in control of education in the United States moved the emphasis in education from the cognitive domain (basics of reading, math, etc.) to the affective domain (social relationships, feelings, etc.). Grade inflation and social promotions began along with a fall in SAT scores. The educational elite said that the "new math" would help the United States to lead the world in the future (similar to Common Core proponents today saying students will have more depth of understanding), but it turned out to be a disaster.

Following the shift away from the basics, NEA president Catherine Barrett in the early 1970s in *Saturday Review of Education* remarked that: "Dramatic changes in the way we will raise our children in the year 2000 are indicated, particularly in terms of schooling. ... We will need to recognize that the so-called 'basic skills,' which currently represent nearly the total effort in elementary schools, will be taught in one-quarter of the present school day. ... When this happens—and it's near—the teacher can rise to his true calling. More than dispenser of information, the teacher will be a conveyor of values, a philosopher. ... We will be agents of change." Furthermore, Carolyn Warner, Arizona State Superintendent of Public Instruction, was quoted in the *Arizona Republic* (January 7, 1975) as saying that "those who educate are more to be honored than those who bear the children. The latter gave them only life, the former teach them the art of living."

In 1972, UNESCO's bestseller *Learning To Be: The World of Education Today and Tomorrow* was published. In this editor work, the authors say they are in search of a "new educational order ... based on scientific and technological training, one of the essential components of scientific humanism." The book also emphasized relativity and dialectical thought, and proclaimed that "... an individual should avoid systematically setting up his beliefs and convictions ... his behavior and customs as models or rules valid for all times."

In the early 1970s, Michael Lerner (who would become an important advisor to Hillary Clinton) authored *The New Socialist Revolution*, in which he proclaimed: "Education will be radically transformed in our socialist community ... the main emphasis will be on learning how to ... live and work collectively. ... The next level is learning some series of skills, for one's first set of jobs." And in Vladimir Turchenko's *The Scientific and Technological Revolution and the Revolution in Education* (1976) imported into the United States is described "linking instruction with productive labor" (this is similar to plank 10 of the *Communist Manifesto* mentioned earlier).

The year after Turchenko's book appears in the United States, on November 17, 1977, U.S. Assistant Secretary of Education Mary Berry delivered an address, "The Chinese Experience in Education: What America Stands to Learn," at the University of Illinois. She revealed that the U.S. Office of Education was developing lifelong learning programs modeled after the communist Chinese programs. Two years later, the U.S. Department of Education (USDOE) was established under President Jimmy Carter, fulfilling a promise he had made to the NEA.

In 1980, Ronald Reagan was elected president, taking office in January 1981. Over the next several years, Carter administration holdovers left the National Institute of Education (within USDOE). One of them, Marc Tucker (an NIE associate director) went to the newly established (early 1985) Carnegie Forum on Education and the Economy (CFEE). This was after North Carolina governor Jim Hunt had written an article in *Phi Delta Kappan* (Fall 1984) advising linking education and the economy, and he suggested to David Hamburg (Carnegie Foundation CEO) that he fund a CFE (and Hunt became vice chairman).

The year after CFEE was begun, Mike Cohen left NIE in 1986 and went to the National Governors Association (NGA). About the same time, Ramsey Selden (who had opposed our efforts to have more intensive systematic phonics taught in schools) left NIE and went to the Council of Chief State School Officers (CCSSO) as one of their lead education personnel. The NGA (of which Hunt has been a chairman) and CCSSO would eventually be the lead organizations promoting Common Core.

In the Winter 1987/88 edition of *Action in Teacher Education,* Professors Martin Haberman and James Collins wrote in "The Future of the Teaching Profession" that

> schooling is now seen primarily as job training and, for this reason, quite comparable to schooling in non-democratic societies. Once education is redefined as a personal good and as emphasizing preparation for the world of work as its first purpose, our schools can appropriately be compared with those of the U.S.S.R.

At the same time as the Haberman/Collins article appeared, the CFEE changed its name to the National Center on Education and the Economy (NCEE) with board members including David Rockefeller, Jr. and Hillary Clinton. Early in 1989, NCEE produced *To Secure Our Future: The Federal Role in Education,* which would play an important role in framing the issues and shaping the agreements that would be made at the Education Summit held at the University of Virginia (Charlottesville) in September 1989.

George H. W. Bush (Skull & Bones member elected president in November 1988) and the governors of the fifty states met at the summit and agreed to establish national education goals. Even though President Bush was a Republican and had many Republican governors from whom to choose, he selected Arkansas governor Bill Clinton (Rhodes scholar) to head the initial work. This is an example of how the power elite manages both the political left and right. In Donna Hearne's *The Long War and Common Core* (2015), she quotes former New Jersey governor Thomas Kean as saying "The Common Core is a descendant of Charlottesville and its aftermath" ("Historic Summit Fueled Push for K-12 Standards," *Education Week,* September 23, 2014).

Following the summit, the NGA would ask members of NCEE's staff to assist in the development of national education goals (six but later eight). This process would culminate in the announcement of national education goals by President George H. W. Bush in his January 31,1990, State of the Union address.

In the summer of 1989, NCEE's board of trustees had created the Commission on the Skills of the American Workforce to study the current and future skill needs of our nation's non-college work-force. The commission then compiled a report, *America's Choice: High Skills Or Low Wages!,* which was released in June 1990.

In February 1990, the U.S. Department of Labor established the Secretary's Commission on Achieving Necessary Skills (SCANS), which was charged with "defining a common core of skills that constitute job readiness in this new economic environment" (note the term "common core," and Governor Hunt would title his pro-gram "JobReady"). In 1992, SCANS issued *Skills and Tasks for Jobs: A SCANS Report for America 2000.* This is an example of why the American people should never let the national elite tell the rest of us what to do. On page 3-199 of the report under Responsibility (F13), it states the following: *"Milk Cows.* To perform this task, the farmer brings cows to a barn early in the morning and sets up milking equipment, and ensures proper operation. The farmer then brings the first cows into the milking parlor and feeds them by attaching milkers. ... Task ID#: 7131631." These "geniuses" actually said you feed cows by attaching milkers to them !

In 1990, NCEE formed the National Alliance for Restruc-turing Education, which had the Industrial Areas Foundation

(IAF, founded by radical Saul Alinsky) produce a concept paper, "Engaging the Public: One Way to Organize." Remember what Alinsky wrote about community organizers "rubbing raw resentments" and "fanning latent hostilities."

On May 23, 1991, the Bush administration presented to Congress the "America 2000 Excellence in Education Act," based on the six (later eight) national education goals and calling for a "national test" based on national standards. Although the test was supposed to be voluntary, the administration urged colleges to consider test results in their admissions decisions and employers to consider them when making hiring decisions.

President Bush's secretary of education from 1991 to 1993 was Lamar Alexander, who endorsed the concept of "a brand new American school" that would be open from six a.m. to six p.m. year-round. He said

> these schools will serve children from age three months to eighteen. That may be a shocking thought to you, but if you were to do an inventory of every baby in your community, and think about what the needs of those babies were for the next four or five years, you might see that those needs might not be served any other way.

Also in 1991, *We Must Take Charge: Our Schools and Our Future,* by Chester Finn was published. Finn had been head of the U.S. Department of Education's Office of Educational Research and Improvement. In the book, not only does Finn advocate a national curriculum, but he also stated that local control "has become an anachronism no longer justified by research, consistent with sound fiscal policy or organizational theory, suited to our mobility patterns, or important to the public." After reading the book, President Bush's secretary of education, Lamar Alexander, told Finn, "You saved me six months" in organizing the president's education initiative.

Likewise in 1991, the "Michigan Model" Common Core Curriculum was introduced. And from July 29 to August 4, teachers from around the country met at Snowmass, Colorado, and produced dozens of performance tasks for students that "are tied to world-class standards that all students will need to meet," according the NCEE's president Marc Tucker. In a press release dated August 5, Colorado governor Roy Romer at Snowmass was quoted as saying that President Bush's proposal for a national student examination could lean heavily on the work of the New Standards Project.

A few months later, in the March 1992 edition of *Educational Leadership*, an article titled "Will America Choose High Skills or Low wages" by Ira Magaziner (Rhodes scholar) and Hillary Clinton was published, in which they referred to President Bush's education initiative, "America 2000," announcing the development of a national examination system for the nation's K-12 school systems.

Hillary Clinton and Ira Magaziner were on the board of NCEE which wanted, according to *A Human Resources Development Plan* (1992), a "national system of education in which curriculum, pedagogy, examinations and teacher education and licensure systems are all linked to the national standards, and the standards are the same everywhere."

Also in 1992, NCEE president Marc Tucker co-authored *Thinking for a Living: Work Skills and Future of the American Economy,* in which he wrote:

> As this is written [1992], the former members of the communist bloc in Eastern Europe and the Soviet Union are setting out to fashion new societies. ... Many of those countries have done a better job than we of building effective human resource development programs, and for that reason, may yet surprise the world in economic prowess.

On August 2, 1992, Assistant Labor Secretary Roberts Jones announced that the federal government was preparing to deny aid and student loans to schools that fail to prepare their graduates with the skills needed to compete for jobs in the modern workplace, saying, "This is a touchy subject."

Three months later, NCEE president Marc Tucker wrote a revealing letter to his board member Hillary Clinton on November 11, 1992, saying he had just come from David Rockefeller, Jr.'s office where they were "celebrating" Bill Clinton's election as president, as that would allow putting into place their agenda to integrate education into a national system of "human resources development ... from cradle to grave ... [for] everyone. ... We propose that Bill [Clinton] take a leaf out of the German book [regarding required] apprenticeship slots."

Relevant to Tucker's letter, American Enterprise Institute senior fellow Lynne Cheney wrote in her April 2, 1997 article "Whose National Standards?" in *The Wall Street Journal*:

> Undersecretary of Education Mike Smith has worked closely with the NCEE. Like Robert Schwartz, then head of educational giving for the Pew Foundation, Mr. Smith was among those whom NCEE president Marc Tucker brought together right after the 1992 election to advise Mrs. Clinton. After the meeting Mr. Tucker wrote an eighteen-page letter to "Dear Hillary" advising that the Clintons aim to "remold the entire American system" of education and training. Crucial to spinning a "seamless web" of education and labor policy that would envelop all Americans "from cradle to grave," Mr. Tucker wrote, are "clear national standards of performance."

The result of the Tucker-Clinton plan was that Tucker's ally at the National Institute of Education (where I worked) within the Office of Educational Research and Improvement (OERI), Mike

Cohen, wrote Goals 2000 for President Clinton's secretary of education Richard Riley, for whom Cohen was a special assistant for several years after working for the National Governors Association (NGA). On April 21, 1993, President Clinton transmitted the "Goals 2000: Educate America Act," to Congress.

Title I of the legislation "codified into law the six [later eight] national goals." Title II of the legislation dealt with national education standards and assessments. And Title IV established a National Skill Standards Board. One of the board members was Carolyn Warner, who as the state superintendent of education for Arizona said that "those who educate are more to be honored than those who bear the children. The latter gave them only life, the former teach them the art of living" (*Arizona Republic,* January 7, 1975).

Commenting on the legislation, Dianne Ravitch (assistant secretary of OERI during the Bush administration) wrote in the May 26, 1993, *New York Times* "Clinton's Math: More Gets Less," in which she stated:

> The Clinton administration's school reform bill would expand dramatically the scope and cost of federal regulation of local schools. ... To satisfy Congressional critics, the Administration revised its bill, laying the foundation for an interventionist Federal role in local schooling. ... At the heart of the bill is a powerful new agency, called the National Education Standards and Improvement Council, which would function like a national school baord. It would certify national curriculum standards, state tests and state "opportunty to learn" standards.

On March 26, 1994, the U.S. Senate passed the legislation (the House passed it earlier), and Goals 2000 became law with eight goals codified, and provision for a National Education Standards and Improvement Council, which would certify "what all students should know and be able to do" and certify "national content and student performance standards." These last provisions amounted to the widely objectionable "outcome-based education," which would later be combined with "school-to-work" to form the basis of Common Core. In 1994, Sen. Ted Kennedy's School-to-Work Opportunities Act also passed Congress.

Mike Cohen mentioned above was "detailed" on June 28,1996, from the U.S. Department of Education to the White House to become President Clinton's advisor on education. In that position, Cohen was able to exert great influence upon the president's February 4, 1997, State of the Union address, in which the president delivered a "Call to Action" concerning education, calling for

> national standards representing what all our students must
> know to succeed in the knowledge economy of the twenty-first
> century. Every state and school must shape the curriculum to
> reflect these standards. ... To help students meet the standards
> and measure their progress, we will lead an effort over the next
> two years to develop national tests of student achieve in reading
> and math.

Commenting on President Clinton's proposed national standards, two months after his State of the Union address, former head of the National Endowment for the Humanities Lynne Cheney wrote: "Whose National Standards?" (*The Wall Street Journal,* April 2, 1997) referring to an earlier attempt to develop national history standards and stating: "Ninety-nine members of the U.S. Senate voted to reject history standards that would have students learning more about Joseph McCarthy than George Washington, more about Indian chief Speckled Snake than about Thomas Edison."

The same is occurring under Common Core (CC) today. College Board (CB) president (and Rhodes scholar) David Coleman announced the thirty-four advanced placement (AP) courses high school students take would be aligned with CC. Now AP teachers must teach the CB's "framework" defining "the required knowledge of each period" in history. The CB website states that "all questions [in the AP exam] are derived from the course's stated objectives." In the "required knowledge" for the American Revolutionary period, there's no Jefferson, Adams, Madison, or Franklin. In the Civil War period, there's no Gettysburg Address. In the World War II period, there's no Hitler, D-Day, or Truman. Regarding the Civil Rights movement, there's no Martin Luther King, Jr., Rosa Parks, etc.

The primary entity promoting CC has been Achieve, which was founded in 1996. Its first president was Robert Schwartz (who had worked at NIE, where I worked), and one of its first co-chairmen (1996–2002) was IBM's former CEO Lewis Gerstner. Shortly after Achieve was founded, Gerstner made an announcement that indicated that he and other CEO's would consider locating/expanding or not their corporations' facilities in a particular place in the U.S. based upon whether the locality or state had adopted Achieve's internationally benchmarked standards!

Relevant to these internationally benchmarked, most people do not realize that CC is part of a much larger international effort. As part of a New Transatlantic Agreement, on May 5–6, 1997, the U.S. and the European Union convened a major conference, "Bridging the Atlantic: People-to-People Links" calling for "thematic networks for curriculum development" and stating that "governments too are obliged to adapt their economic, training and social welfare programs." The "Partners in a Global Economy Working Group" of the conference discussed "what redesigning of curricula is required … (i.e., what career skills are needed). … "

At this time, on the National Skill Standards Board website was mention of a report by the Tavistock Institute for the European Commission. The report was completed in October 1997 and described the relevancy of Goals 2000, SCANS typology with its "profound implications for the curriculum and training changes that this will require" and what skills standards and portable credentials "benchmarked to international standards. ... "

As the movement toward global education increased, George W. Bush was elected president, taking office in 2001, and his secretary of education, Rod Paige on October 3, 2003, in Paris stated: "The United States is pleased to return to UNESCO. ... Our governments have entrusted us with the responsibility of preparing our children to become citizens of the world." President Obama would later refer to himself as a citizen of the world, but the problem with this concept, as opposed to resident or inhabitant of the world, is that "citizenship" entails legal obligations. And world citizenship obligations would trump those of national citizenship.

On November 17, 2004, at UNESCO's headquarters in Paris, UNESCO signed a twenty-six-page "Cooperation Agreement" with Microsoft (Bill Gates founder and CEO) to develop a "master curriculum" for teacher training and information technologies based on standards, guidelines, benchmarks and assessment techniques. Gates initialed every page and agreed that this curriculum was to reflect UNESCO's values. These values were explained in first UNESCO director-general Sir Julian Huxley's *UNESCO: Its Purpose and Its Philosophy* as including "a scientific world humanism, global in extent and evolutionary in background" with "transfer of full sovereignty from separate nations to a world organization ... political unification in some sort of world government would be required. ... "

The next year (2005), Bill Gates funded the New Commission on the Skills of the American Workforce (created by NCEE president Marc Tucker). And in 2008, the Bill and Melinda Gates Foundation funded the International Benchmarking Advisory Group report for CC standards on behalf of the National Governors Association (NGA), Council of Chief State School Officers, and Achieve titled "Benchmarking for Success: Ensuring U.S. Students

Receive a World-Class Education" showing the U.N. is a member of the Common Core Advisory Group (also see "How Bill Gates pulled off the Common Core revolution" in *The Washington Post*, June 8, 2014).

Concerning Achieve, in January 2003 Mike Cohen had become the new head of this organization. He had been director of education policy at the NGA (1986–1990), director of the National Alliance for Restructuring Education (1990–1993), and senior advisor to U.S. Secretary of Education Richard Riley under President Clinton. He was detailed to the White House from 1996 to 1999, and then became U.S. Assistant Secretary of Education for Elementary and Secondary Education (1999–2001). Under Cohen, Achieve "formed the Partnership for the Assessment of College and Career Readiness (PARCC), one of the two organizations developing common assessments, and helped develop Common Core State Standards" (see www.achieve.org/michael-cohen).

The next major step in the development of CC occurred in June 2008 when the NGA co-hosted an education forum with the Hunt Institute (a project of former North Carolina governor James B. Hunt, Jr.—see my NewsWithViews columns regarding Jim Hunt as an agent of the power elite, PE). This was followed by the June 1, 2009, release of a report that forty-six states had joined a "State-Led Process to Develop a Common Core of Standards."

The NGA, CCSSO and Achieve had already issued their own report calling for national education standards, and although the process of developing the standards is advertised as "state-led," the license agreement with says: "NGA/CCSSO shall be acknowledged as the sole owners and developers of the Common Core State Standards." In case you think this means the NGA and CCSSO take responsibility for the results of CC, the license goes on to say in capital letters:

THE COMMON CORE STATE STANDARDS ARE PROVIDED AS-IS AND

WITH ALL FAULTS, AND NGA CENTER/CCSSO MAKE NO REPRE-
SENTATIONS OR WARRANTIES OF ANY KIND, EXPRESS, IMPLIED,
STATUTORY OR OTHERWISE, INCLUDING, WITHOUT LIMITATION,
WARRANTIES OF TITLE, MERCHANTIBILITY (SIC), FITNESS FOR A
PARTICULAR PURPOSE, NONINFRIGEMENT, ACCURACY, OR THE
PRESENCE OR ABSENCE OF ERRORS, WHETHER OR NOT DISCOV-
ERABLE. ... UNDER NO CIRCUMSTANCES SHALL NGA CENTER OR
CCSSO, INDIVIDUALLY OR JOINTLY, BE LIABLE FOR ANY DIRECT,
INDIRECT, INCIDENTAL, SPECIAL, EXEMPLARY, CONSEQUENTIAL,
OR PUNITIVE DAMAGES HOWEVER CAUSED AND ON ANY LEGAL
THEORY OF LIABILITY, WHETHER FOR CONTRACT, TORT, STRICT
LIABILITY, OR A COMBINATION THEREOF (INCLUDING NEGLI-
GENCE OR OTHERWISE) ARISING IN ANY WAY OUT OF THE USE
OF THE COMMON CORE STATE STANDARDS, EVEN IF ADVISED OF
THE POSSIBILITY OF SUCH RISK AND POTENTIAL DAMAGE WITH-
OUT LIMITING THE FOREGO LICENSEE WAIVES THE RIGHT TO
SEEK LEGAL REDRESS AGAINST, AND RELEASES FROM ALL LIABIL-
ITY AND COVENANTS NOT TO SUE, NGA CENTER AND CCSSO.

Entering the picture at this time is Sir Michael Barber, placing CC
in a global setting (even the Programme for International Student
Assessment is being aligned with CC). In May 2010, he founded
the U.S. Education Delivery Institute, which formed a partnership with Achieve to provide leadership training for CC. Barber
also became the leader for the PARCC consortium. So who is Sir
Michael Barber? He is the chief education officer for the Pearson
Foundation which has offices in over seventy nations. Pearson has
taken over many education publishing companies (e.g., the education divisions of HarperCollins, Simon & Schuster, Addison-
Wesley Longman, etc.). Barber majored in history at Oxford University and taught in Zimbabwe (formerly Rhodesia), and is no
doubt familiar with Cecil Rhodes. In November 2012, he began
the Learning Curve for Pearson, but it was commissioned by *The*

*Economist* (magazine) Intelligence Unit (which has connections with MI6, British Intelligence). Jeb Bush is a leading candidate (and PE favorite) in the 2016 presidential race, and Pearson has been a top corporate sponsor of Bush's education foundation.

According to author Orlean Koehle in *The Hidden C's of Common Core*, there are five lead writers for the CC assessments, none of whom has any K–12 classroom teaching experience in the subjects for which they prepared the assessments. Two of these, College Board head (since 2012) David Coleman in English and Jason Zimba in math, are Rhodes scholars (remember Cecil Rhodes and his secret Society of the Elect "to take the government of the whole world" wanted to penetrate four main areas, one of which was education). Coleman and Zimba had gone to Chicago with their New York organization The Grow Network to produce data studies for the Chicago Annenberg Challenge (CAC) with board member Barack Obama, who had been recruited there by radical Bill Ayers (Obama was CAC's first chairman and Ayers co-chairman, serving together for eight years). Although CC is advertised as promoting high standards, Zimba speaking before the Massachusetts Department of Education (March 2010) admitted that the CC math standards would only prepare students for a minimum junior college level (see Koehle or www.youtube.com/watch?v=eJZY4mh2rt8). For one thing, CC defers algebra until ninth grade, which makes it difficult to complete calculus in high school and therefore more difficult to get in the better colleges.

On February 19, 2014, National Education Association president Dennis Van Roekel posted a letter on NEAToday.org stating:

> Seven of ten teachers believe that implementation of the standards is going poorly in their schools. Worse yet, teachers report that there has been little to no attempt to allow educators to share what's needed to get [CC] implementation right.

In fact, two-thirds of all teachers report that they have not even been asked how to implement these new standards in their classrooms."

Two months later, on Stephen Colbert's April 8, 2014, TV show, he said:

I have long opposed Obama's Common Core education curriculum that sets uniform standards across all the States. Different states have different values. I don't want my kids ending up on Colorado's drug educatin course that classifies weed as a condiment. As much as I didn't expect it, I may be coming around to the Common Core, as it turns out Common Core testing prepares our youth for what they will face as adults, constant stress and confusion ... and passive, aggression note taking.

He later gives an example of a second grader explaining how he got a math answer. The child wrote: "I got the answer by talking in my brain and I agreed with the answer that my brain got."

David Coleman's intent is to align his College Board SATs to CC (see *The New York Times*, March 5, 2014). In Coleman's English portion of the SAT, challenging words like "depreciatory" have been removed to align with the lower standards of CC. So if CC is not about higher standards, what purpose does Coleman serve? In the past, parents have been able to opt out of faddish education reform movements (e.g., outcome-based education), but with Coleman aligning the SATs with CC, even private, religious, or home-schooling parents will have to align their assessments with CC if they want their children to score well on the SATs and get into a good college.

But CC isn't just about English, math, history, etc. It is also about changing values. For example, the mother of an eight-year-old girt in Louisiana said her daughter had been assigned homework about adultery, and the teacher said she got the assignment from CC materials for third graders (Scripps Media, October 20, 2013).

CC is also about data collection. In "Push Against CC Gains Momentum" (*Education Reporter,* May 2013), one reads:

> CC gains unprecedented access to students' personal information to schools and third parties. ... The Obama administration made changes to the Family Rights and Privacy Act, broadening the collection of students' information and sharing it with other agencies. This information will not only be available to schools, but also to researchers and private companies. ... 'Turning massive amounts of personal data about public school students [over] to a private corporation without any public input is profoundly disturbing and irresponsible,' the executive director of the New York Civil Liberties Union told the *Daily News.* The Electronic Privacy Information Center in Washington is suing the U.S. Department of Education in an effort to stop the illegal collection, storage, and sharing of student data (3-13-13).

Some states have had second thoughts about CC and have developed their own standards and assessments. Unfortunately, they often still align them with CC, so their high school students can score well on the SAT which is aligned with CC.

At this point, you may be wondering what is so bad about the CC assessments. Sandra Stotsky and James Milgram were members of a national validation committee asked to sign off on CC in 2010, but they did not, with Stotsky criticizing the English/language arts standards and Milgram characterizing the methods for solving math problems as convoluted. As an example of CC's convoluted math, the simple addition of 29 plus 17 to equal 46 becomes the following: 29 is changed to 20 plus 9, and 17 is changed to 10 plus 7. The 20 and 10 are added to make 30, and the 9 and 7 are added to make 16. The 16 becomes 10 plus 6, and the 10 is added to the 30 to make 40, which is added to the 6 to make 46.

Stotsky explained that the CC standards are really skill sets that will lower the academic level of what seve ty percent of students study, replacing a good deal of classical literature with informational texts. Concerning math, child clinical psychologist Dr. Megan Koschnick explained that CC's practices require student "reason abstractly" beginning in kindergarten, but she pointed out that children cannot engage in abstract thinking until age eleven or twelve!

In "Making Math Education Even Worse" (*The Wall Street Journal*, August 5, 2014), National Academy of Sciences award-winning University of California at Berkeley math professor emeritus Marina Ratner wrote:

> The Common Core standards were several years behind the old [California] standards. … [The] requirement of visual models and creating stories is all over the Common Core. The students were constantly told to draw models to answer trivial questions such as finding twenty percent of eighty. … This model-drawing mania went on in my grandson's class for the entire year, leaving no time to cover geometry and other important topics. … The most astounding statement I have read is the claim that Common Core standards are "internationally benchmarked." They are not. The Common Core fails any comparison with the standards of high-achieving countries. … They are lower in the total scope of learned material, in the depth and rigor of the treatment of mathematical subjects, and in the delayed and often inconsistent and incoherent introductions of mathematical concepts and skills. … The Common Core standards will move the U.S. even closer the bottom in international ranking.

And Carol Burris, New York State's 2013 high school principal of the year, reported that as a result of CC, "We see kids [who] don't want to go to school anymore." Regarding CC math, Ms. Burris remarked: "I fear that they are creating a generation of young students who are learning to hate mathematics" (*The New York Times*, February 17, 2014).

If you look at George Washington University's Center for Education Policy report in the February 10, 2015, "Compendium of Research on the Common Core State Standards" (www.cep-dc.org), you will see that in an evaluation of sixty pieces of research used to support CC, there is no evidence to support the claim that CC standards will improve student achievement. The beauty of the American educational system in the past was that the fifty states were like fifty laboratories. And if one state developed new teaching methods or activities that improved academic achievement, other states could voluntarily adopt them. However, there was no "one size fits all," top-down directed, standards-based assessments such as CC has, and which Americans should reject.